The Best
Men's Stage Monologues
of 1997

Other books by Jocelyn A. Beard

100 Men's Stage Monologues from the 1980s

100 Women's Stage Monologues from the 1980s

The Best Men's/Women's Stage Monologues of 1990

The Best Men's/Women's Stage Monologues of 1991

The Best Men's/Women's Stage Monologues of 1992

The Best Men's/Women's Stage Monologues of 1993

The Best Men's/Women's Stage Monologues of 1994

The Best Men's/Women's Stage Monologues of 1995

The Best Men's/Women's Stage Monologues of 1996

The Best Stage Scenes for Men from the 1980s

The Best Stage Scenes for Women from the 1980s

The Best Stage Scenes of 1992

The Best Stage Scenes of 1993

The Best Stage Scenes of 1994

The Best Stage Scenes of 1995

The Best Stage Scenes of 1996

The Best Stage Scenes of 1997

Monologues from Classic Plays 468 B.C. to 1960 A.D.

Scenes from Classic Plays 468 B.C. to 1970 A.D.

100 Great Monologues from the Renaissance Theatre

100 Great Monologues from the Neo-Classical Theatre

100 Great Monologues from the 19th C. Romantic & Realistic Theatre

Smith and Kraus *Books For Actors*
THE MONOLOGUE SERIES

The Best Men's / Women's Stage Monologues of 1997
The Best Men's / Women's Stage Monologues of 1996
The Best Men's / Women's Stage Monologues of 1995
The Best Men's / Women's Stage Monologues of 1994
The Best Men's / Women's Stage Monologues of 1993
The Best Men's / Women's Stage Monologues of 1992
The Best Men's / Women's Stage Monologues of 1991
The Best Men's / Women's Stage Monologues of 1990
One Hundred Men's / Women's Stage Monologues from the 1980's
2 Minutes and Under: Character Monologues for Actors
Street Talk: Character Monologues for Actors
Uptown: Character Monologues for Actors
Ice Babies in Oz: Character Monologues for Actors
Monologues from Contemporary Literature: Volume I
Monologues from Classic Plays
100 Great Monologues from the Renaissance Theatre
100 Great Monologues from the Neo-Classical Theatre
100 Great Monologues from the 19th C. Romantic and Realistic Theatres
A Brave and Violent Theatre: 20th C. Irish Monologues, Scenes & Hist. Context
Kiss and Tell: Restoration Monologues, Scenes and Historical Context
The Great Monologues from the Humana Festival
The Great Monologues from the EST Marathon
The Great Monologues from the Women's Project
The Great Monologues from the Mark Taper Forum

YOUNG ACTOR SERIES

Great Scenes and Monologues for Children
Great Monologues for Young Actors
Multicultural Monologues for Young Actors

SCENE STUDY SERIES

Scenes From Classic Plays 468 B.C. to 1960 A.D.
The Best Stage Scenes of 1997
The Best Stage Scenes of 1996
The Best Stage Scenes of 1995
The Best Stage Scenes of 1994
The Best Stage Scenes of 1993
The Best Stage Scenes of 1992
The Best Stage Scenes for Men / Women from the 1980's

If you require pre-publication information about upcoming Smith and Kraus books, you may receive our semi-annual catalogue, free of charge, by sending your name and address to *Smith and Kraus Catalogue, 4 Lower Mill Road, North Stratford, NH 03590. Or call us at (800) 895-4331, fax (603) 922-3348.*

The Best
Men's Stage Monologues
of 1997

edited by Jocelyn A. Beard

The Monologue Audition Series

SK
A Smith and Kraus Book

Published by Smith and Kraus, Inc.
One Main Street, Lyme, NH 03768

First Edition: August 1998
10 9 8 7 6 5 4 3 2

The Monologue Audition Series ISSN 1067-134X

NOTE: These monologues are intended to be used for audition and class study; permission is not required to use the material for those purposes. However, if there is a paid performance of any of the monologues included in this book, please refer to the permissions acknowledgment pages to locate the source who can grant permission for public performance.

Contents

Preface

1997 was a humdinger of a theatrical season which found many playwrights writing hell-bent for leather. (I have no idea what that really means, but I love the way it sounds.) If one were to have the effrontery—as I often do—to divide the season's offerings into different genres, the standouts in my opinion would be the healthy crop of slick adaptations of classics such as *Alki, Epic Poetry, The Government Inspector, Polaroid Stories* and *Narcissus And Echo.* All of these clever plays contain great monologues which offer the actor the opportunity to play larger-than-life characters. This may be a welcome respite to those of you bored to tears with the plethora of whiny "Don't Hate Me Because I'm a Man and You're Not" roles that have sadly become the hallmark of late 1990s dramatic writing.

Weird, intense on the edge monologues for those of you who one day hope to dethrone Christopher Walken may be found in *Bafo, Carpool, Good Guys Wear Yellow, Icarus, Hazing The Monkey, Manson, Reading The Mind Of God, The Pharmacist's Daughter* and *The Sister Upstairs.* Proceed with caution guys, these characters are out there, but gar-un-teed to get the director's attention.

Somewhat more comedic material for those who believe it's best to leave 'em laughing (or at the very least not crying) may be found in *The Government Inspector, A Night At The Blowhole, Narcissus & Echo, Stars,* and *"Dusk"* from *By The Sea By The Sea By The Beautiful Sea.*

Good solid dramatic monologues of a four-square variety are found in *Bafo, A Body Not Greatly Changed, The Maiden's Prayer, Wedding Dance, Easter, The Golem, In Search Of The*

Red River Dog, What Cats Know, Patchwork, Private Eyes, Soul Survivor, and *To Each His Own.*

Young performers (age twenty and under) should check out *Daddy And The Tunnel Rat, The Legacy, Molly's Delicious, Polaroid Stories, Soda Fountain* and *Sticky And Shary.*

Material for mature actors (age fifty and up) may be found in *Autumn Canticle, The Confession of Many Strangers, The Golem, Jack Flew, Manson, Unpacking Dominic's Trunk, War Monologue,* and *Whiteout.*

My personal favorite in this collection is the monologue from Joan Ackerman's *Marcus Is Walking.* This may someday go down in theatrical history as the most romantic monologue of all time. I know...I'm sappy, but hey, if you're auditioning for a woman director in springtime I suggest you give it a try!

This book is dedicated to all the romantic saps who refuse to knuckle-under to pre-millennial nihilism.

The Brickhouse
Patterson, New York...the pride of the Harlem Valley
Spring 1998

Alki

Eric Overmeyer

Scene: the Puget Sound Territory, 1851

Serio-Comic
Peer: (20s) an imaginative young scalawag

> *When the girl that he fancied for himself is about to be married to another, Peer spies on the wedding festivities from a hill above the town and daydreams about becoming a pirate.*

PEER: There's a stagecoach. And there's a steam engine, puffing across the prairie. And there's a clipper ship, out of San Francisco—bound for Rio 'round the Cape Horn. Look at the sails on that one! And there's Peer—Captain Peer to you, swabbie, dressed in a blue and gold uniform, brass buttons, and gold braid and a captain's hat! Yes, sir! There's Captain Peer, standing on the quarterdeck, issuing orders. Captain Peer, the Pirate King! Scourge of the Spanish Main! Arrrrggg! A parrot on one shoulder and a patch over one eye, which Captain Peer lost in the sack of Panama, 'case you're curious, in an epic duel across the parapets, waged under the blazing Caribbean sun before thousands of onlookers, just Captain Peer and the Spanish Commander, the shouts of the crowd, the clash of steel, swords flashing in the sun, clothing slashed to ribbons, back and forth they duel for hours, thrust and parry, blood streaming from a hundred, no, a thousand wounds, large and small, and Captain Peer, distracted momentarily by a comely smile from a breathtakingly beautiful senorita on a balcony strewn with roses, Captain Peer, ever the gallant gentleman, tips his hat to pay his respects and consequently stumbles on the cobblestones, the Spanish Commander flicks the tip of his blade, so—and catches the Captain's eye and slits it across, blood gushes from the socket, the crowd gasps, grows silent, surely this is the end, Captain Peer staggers, stumbles, stays on his feet, retreats, the Spanish Commander smells victory, presses in for the kill, Muerto! Muerto! he cries, slashing furiously with his saber, Captain Peer blocks the blows, desperate, his vision cloudy, the pain intense, searing, the sun dazzling, the sky spinning, the Spanish Commander backs Captain Peer up against a white-washed stone wall, pauses a moment, and prepares to deliver the coup de grace, the crowd stunned and silent, the only sound under the merciless sun the labored breathing of the two swashbuckling combatants—the Spanish Commander crosses himself, and then he lunges, the crowd roars, a hoarse cry goes up from ten thousand throats, Captain Peer dodges the blow, the blade pierces his side but misses his heart, and Peer parries, like this and that and thus and so—and stabs his sword square through the Spanish Commander's neck—and sends him straight to God! And the crowd erupts like a Roman candle! Explodes! Runs amok! Goes hog wild and dances fandangoes in the streets! Frenzy! Chaos! Church bells and cannon fire! Flowers and hats fill the air! Never have they seen such a fight! Such bravery! Such swordsmanship! Such panache! They pick Captain Peer up and put him on their shoulders and carry him to the plaza, where they tend his wounds. And the most beautiful senorita in Panama, in the Caribbean, in the whole of the Western Hemisphere perhaps, she who favored him with a smile from the balcony strewn with roses and so caused him to lose his footing, this very same senorita insists on stanching his wounds and mopping his brow and lifting the water ladle to his parched lips. And she smiles her incomparable smile, and he thinks it well worth the loss of an eye. A mere eye. Small price to pay for such a smile. And she stays with him through the sultry night, which is filled with the scent of jasmine and the cries of nightingales and peacocks. And in the morning he's well enough to travel, and she accompanies him back to his ship, and the trade winds billow the sails, and they lift anchor and set sail for a desert isle of flowers and coconut palms, and together they count out a fortune in Spanish gold and jewels, while she strums a guitar and sings a gypsy ballad. *(He falls silent, daydreaming, lost in reverie.)* They still talk about it. Down in Panama. 'Case you didn't know.

Alki

Eric Overmeyer

Scene: the Puget Sound Territory, 1851

Serio-Comic
Peer: (20s) an imaginative young scalawag

> *Peer has stolen Ingrid from her wedding and is subsequently chased into the woods by an angry posse. In the forest, Ingrid is forgotten as Peer is seduced by a band of feral girls. The following morning Peer awakes on the cold earth feeling much the worse for wear.*

PEER: Oh, my head! It hurts! Damn! Every vein throbs. I think I have a fever. I hear bells. The light is so beautiful. Like roses. The mountains look like icy castles. Now they're on fire. I must lie down. Oh, my aching head. *(He lies down.)* Did I really steal a bride and carry her away into the mountains? A posse howling at my heels? Did I really leave the bride behind and spend a day and a night frolicking with three wild women of the mountains? Like to wear a man out, those three. Kill him with kindness. Seems like a dream. Must have been a lie. A tall tale. A damn lie and a damn shame. Oh, my head hurts! I'm seeing things. Those shadows look like soldiers— *(He looks upwards.)* There's a pair of eagles soaring over yonder gorge. Wonder where they're going? Look at them. Free. Free as a bird, that's what they say. And I'm stuck here on the ground, with all my trials and tribulations. *(He gets to his feet.)* I can do like them eagles. Soar like that. Ride the four winds. Go where fortune and fancy take me. The girls I leave behind will wait in vain for my return. Pace along the widow walk. Scan the horizon. Pine away. I won't be back. The four winds, the seven seas. I will know them like most men know their front parlor. *(Stares out.)* Funny. That cloud there looks like my granddaddy's farm. Like it was when it was first hacked out of the howling wilderness and wrought like Spanish silver into something fine. Not the sorry heap of scraps it is now, but shining and new, full of light and music and people laughing. There's a party, a celebration! A new-born boy! They drink his health! To Peer, my daddy says! To Peer! All the leading citizens of the Territory gather round and drink to me! To my future! To Peer! Whose daddy was a dandy! To Peer! Born of a great family! And destined for fame and fortune!

(Lightning crackles, thunder claps. Peer stands on the precipice, arms outstretched.)

PEER: Peer Gynt! Peer Gynt! Peer Gynt!

(A bolt of lightning hits him, knocks him out cold.)

Autumn Canticle

John W. Lowell

Scene: the atelier of a Tudor-style house in Croton, NY. Autumn 1972

Dramatic
David: (50s) a successful concert vocalist

> *David's long-time companion, Peter, has lost his passion for musical composition and has suffered a recent heart-attack. Walker, a younger man who has wandered into their lives, seems to have a beneficial effect on Peter and is encouraging him to write a book as he recuperates. David soon becomes jealous of Walker's influence on Peter and here confronts the younger man with his concerns.*

DAVID: Did you know I wanted to be a composer? That can be part of my biographical footnote in your book. David Williams: Composer. Hard to believe? It's true. I happily spare you for the moment that particular honor. But I warn you, the manuscripts do exist—somewhere. Oh, when I was young I composed all sorts of music; piano pieces, a ten-minute symphony, a string quartet. My work was precocious and impressive, that's what everybody said. I applied to Curtis and I dazzled the faculty with my talents. I was so damned good I knew I was on my way to being—well, being part of that pantheon you talk about. That's what I thought. As luck would have it I met Peter on the very first day of our very first theory class. I saw him and I was instantly in love with him—who wouldn't've been? He was handsome, and charmingly awkward, and unpretentious, and his smile was warm enough to thaw even the most jaded, frozen soul—which certainly was my soul at eighteen. On that very day I asked him out for coffee, he accepted, and I've rarely let him out of my sight since. So it's all been happiness, and love ever-after, and apart from the romance of it, you can't figure out why the Hell I'm telling you this. Because even that very first day, Peter permitted me to hear *his* music. He played and sang through his marvelous songs and he made me jealous with his facility, with his funny, wonderful improvisations, and then I realized it was preposterous—I was preposterous. I was as much a composer as the typesetter is the novelist. He hadn't intended to, but Peter rebuked my music with every note of his. I had facility. I even had talent. But I didn't have that special—courage—he had even from the very start. The courage to say something—even at the risk of saying it wrong. That's a special courage. He had that courage. I didn't. Disaster! I was lucky, though. I could sing. Without missing a beat I transformed myself; David Williams, creator; David Williams, performer—Billings' performer, primarily. And for us it's been a beautiful partnership. He's written so much for me—too much, so the learned critics would have it. He even wrote *The Gilded Age* for me—and I assure you that experience was as severe a trial of love and honesty as any I would ever wish to undergo. He struggled for years trying to write it. Then Stinko The Greek got his hands on it and he directed that first and only production with all the restraint of a horny adolescent in the back seat of a Buick. The opera premiered and the sky fell in. Since that horrible night all we've had from my dearest friend is a fitful, unhappy silence. Then along comes young Walker who finds, in poor, bereft Peter something to help him fill his days. Thank you, young Walker. I gave up my music—but I can't so easily let him give up his. You're driving him further and further from what I need and I cannot stand that.

Autumn Canticle

John W. Lowell

Scene: the atelier of a Tudor-style house in Croton, NY. Autumn 1972

Dramatic
Peter: (50s) a former musical prodigy now ailing and played-out

> *Peter has had to cope with the loss of his passion for music as well as the disintegration of his body. When his long-time relationship with David, his heart and soul mate, is threatened, he reacts with fear and longing.*

PETER: You can't kill what's already dead. How can I make you understand. What can I—? Think about it. You, with your pinched upper register, and your imperfect pitch, you can still sing, you have your voice. I don't have my voice anymore. I have a big, black, silent nothing. Listen to me, David, I've searched every part of myself to find an idea worth committing to paper. There aren't any. The opera failed was four thousand bars of arid noise and what hurt so much was I knew it all along and I knew I couldn't do any better. But I couldn't stop. I had to finish it. I was afraid—of losing you. I knew composing it was the only way to keep you. And even that inspirational fear didn't make a difference—nothing was making my work better. You haven't any idea how terrifying it is to bring something into the world you hate. And I grew to hate that Goddamned opera. And I've hated everything I've done since. I remember when it used to be I could make one note follow the next with the complete, happy certainty I had done it right. And there were more notes to come. My head was so full of ideas I couldn't get them out fast enough. Then one day the head wasn't quite so full, and the ideas seemed weak, manufactured. Corrupt. From then on, everything I did was artificial and forced into existence. I couldn't do it anymore—not even for you. And God! I wanted to. Well, I had so much at stake—I had you to lose. And I was right, after all, wasn't I? I've lost you. *(Smiling.)* Once upon a time, we were terrific. We were young and talented and it was all going to be a parade of gorgeous triumphs. When I was twenty all I thought about was how much I wanted to grow old with you. Life has a perverse sense of humor, because I got exactly what I wished for. I grew old and I did it with you. Only you didn't grow old with me. And we both knew it. You saw what was happening and you adjusted. You're a remarkable man, David. Most people would have mourned, I think. But it wouldn't be seemly for you to actually leave me like this so you've stayed, and the days have rolled on, and then I'm sick, and then it's out of your hands. You've been marking time until I was safely away and you could be brave in front of a suitably moved audience—you are the ultimate trooper!

Bafo
Best and Final Offer

Tom Strelich

Scene: the conference room of a small defense contractor in the declining Southern California defense/aerospace industry

Dramatic
Sayles: (30–40) an aggressive and optimistic player on the project team

> *Sayles and his co-workers are hard at work on what may be their final project. As they ponder the unknown threat to their continued employment, Sayles explodes with frustration and anger.*

SAYLES: Any paranoid asshole can identify a threat. But to identify everything as a threat, that shows perspective, that shows an understanding of the problem, that shows long-term vision, that shows value-added. That's giving the SPO a flexible, scaleable, expandable, distributed threat that they can use to justify additional funds and guarantee their existence—that's job security for them and us. *(Snowballing.)* It's not like when you were a blue-suiter, when you had the luxury of a single enemy, and money up the ass. When your kids could go to public schools and didn't have to learn about condoms and the dangers of unprotected anal sex, and you could buy a five bedroom house for eighteen thousand dollars, with a pool! Do you know how much a 5 bedroom house costs now? Do you know how much a goddamn private school costs now? *(Collecting himself.)* We are the incumbent contractor, this job is ours to lose, and everybody's coming after us. This is a must-win proposal, and I'm the capture manager, *(Re-snowballing.)* and I've got to get the best out of silverbacks like you and propeller-heads like him *(Willie Peet.)* and

9

chin-pullers like Ashe and I've got to make it all happen. Because if I don't, we're all beached. I know it's not a big threat to you, *(Clay.)* you've got your Air Force retirement to cover your nut. But for the rest of us, it's living in a car and eating out of dumpsters. So don't tell me about threats, I know about threats, I'm the fucking threat manager, and there's only one that really matters...a decline in goddamn life style!

Bafo
Best and Final Offer

Tom Strelich

Scene: the conference room of a small defense contractor in the declining Southern California defense/aerospace industry

Dramatic
P.K.: (30–40) a disgruntled former employee toting a loaded AK-47.

> *P.K. has burst into the offices of the company from which he was recently fired, and he is loaded for bear. After shooting at several people, he corners his former co-workers in a conference room. P.K. takes a moment to survey the project they have been working on and then advises them that they have failed to identify the threat to their work, a mandatory function for corporate survival. Here, he offers them chilling insight into the necessity of being fearful.*

P.K.: Where's the threat? *(Pause, turns to face them.)* Is history wasted on you? Haven't you learned anything? You haven't got a prayer. Unless you have a threat. Don't you remember? Why our knuckle-dragging forefathers picked up that first blunt instrument? Why they painted their faces and put antlers on their heads and did the hokey pokey around the camp fire? *(No response.)* Because they were afraid of something: lightning, thunder, saber tooth tiger. They had a threat. A real, credible, undeniable threat. So they had a need. Before Jesus, before Mohammed, before Jehovah, before the pagan gods, demigods, animal gods, before all the great protectors, you had one, single unifying force in the space-time continuum… *(Turning to them.)* And you *know* what it is? Don't you.

   [They all stare at P.K. motionless.]

P.K.: That's right, the boogeyman. We didn't start praying out of joy or gratitude, but because we were scared shitless. All of mankind's accomplishments, religion, art, civilization, *(Pointing at a commemorative photo.)* I-C-B-M's that go bump in the night— all sprouts from the same seed. When the archangels appeared before the shepherds in a blinding light a hundred generations ago and told them that Jesus Christ, the Son of man, the blessed redeemer, was being born that very night. Did they rise up and weep for joy at the gift to mankind of salvation and eternal life? Heck no. They shrank back in fright and fell on their bellies in sup-plication and submission, and begged for mercy. People back then knew what to do when in the presence of a terrifying, but possibly benevolent, entity. What would people do nowadays if an avenging angel or a burning bush, say, appeared before them? Probably nothing. Probably just say, "wow" and wait for Connie Toyota and News Team Eleven to show up. Nothing makes us fall on our bellies anymore. Only one of these goddamn things *(The AK-47.)* ...not that I'm suggesting. But you would if I asked, right?

[They all silently nod "yes."]

P.K.: This is my point. Threat comes before everything. Because life itself is a threat—do you see the cosmic unity of that, the indivis-ible duality—its very existence, threatens its loss—this has been such an illuminating day for me, everybody should do this. *(Beat.)* You haven't got a PRAYER if you haven't got FAITH. And you can't have FAITH *(Shaking his gun.)* unless you have a THREAT!

[Ashe hiccups noisily.]

P.K.: *(Looking at Ashe, calmly.)* Remember DIE-VAD? Division level Air Defense, or something like that? *(Laughs at the thought.)* That BAFO we worked on over Christmas back during Reagan? You had hiccups like, the whole time. Very annoying. If I had a gun, I woulda shot ya right then...

[Ashe turns and vomits noisily into the trashcan.]

P.K.: *(Looking at Ashe, disapproving.)* Well, I wouldn't call this progress. *(Beat.)* It's a figure of speech, you're overreacting. *(Looks up at the ceiling, points.)* You see that?

[Everyone (except Ashe) looks up at the ceiling.]

P.K.: See that little ding up there? *(P.K. climbs up onto the table, and points to a spot on the ceiling.)* Champagne cork from the DIE-VAD victory party. *(Looking closely at the ding.)* I climbed up here and circled it with a red pen… *(Reading.)* DIE-VAD win, April 17th, late Pleistocene… *(Looks down at them.)* We were lost. We were dead. But we won it on BAFO. Hiccups and everything, we won it on BAFO. Salvation, redemption, resurrection, all rolled up together in our best and final offer. So, you see, there's still hope for you, but you've got a lot of work to do here. And so what I want to know is, "what's *your* best and final offer?" *(P.K. holds the video camera up to his eye, aims at Sayles.)*

Bafo
Best and Final Offer

Tom Strelich

Scene: the conference room of a small defense contractor in the declining Southern California defense/aerospace industry

Dramatic
Clay: (50s) a retired Colonel now employed in the defense industry

> *When he and his co-workers are taken hostage by an ex-employee brandishing a loaded AK-47, the stress of the situation enables this otherwise cool and collected commander of men to make the following confession.*

CLAY: *(Laughs.)* Disneyland!…

[They stop and look at Clay who stands calmly, alone, flat-footed—like a Mexican singer.]

CLAY: Disneyland…Took the wife, kiddies, the whole pack. Stayed at the Disneyland hotel, brand-new back then, still smelled like paint. Nobody cared. We stormed that little room, threw the bags on the floor, pillows in the air, yanked back the curtains and there it was—the Matterhorn, monorail, primeval world, the future. Buck was jumping on the bed. All arms and legs and smiles with no front teeth, looking out the window at that beckoning promise. And I stood there watching him rise and fall. Each little triumph over gravity, each little glimpse of Disneyland made him bigger. I thought we were going to pop and I said, "Boy, you know, Buck, it just doesn't get any better than this, does it?" He looked at me, and time stood still. And everything a father has ever said to a son, and everything a son has ever said to a father was said in that instant. I asked him about it a coupla years back. Asked him if he remembered the incident, that instant we shared. He didn't. He didn't remember much of anything really. Not even me. He was all hollowed out, fading away in a hospice with a buncha other queers, surrounded by those creepy, non-judgmental-superior-acting-public-radio listening Unitarians. He was a faggot and he paid the price, but I loved that boy to the core. And it doesn't matter that he couldn't remember. Even if I forgot it, even if I died never thinking of it again, never acknowledged—it still happened. That moment, between two people, happened in this Universe. You only get one or two truly happy moments in a lifetime, and they never come when you'd expect. You could be walking across a parking lot, or sitting in a car tuning the radio, or making a sandwich on a Saturday afternoon, drinking from a garden hose, or bouncing on a bed at the Disneyland hotel, when it hits you with undeniable, overwhelming force—it doesn't get any better than this! And the miracle is that this flawed, finite, fucked-up little bag of protoplasm saw that, felt that, knew that. And nothing can take that from me, not a bullet, not bad news from the lab, not a Goddamn boogey man! So you can take your best and final offer and shove it up your ass! You're not a threat to me now, I'm not in this body anymore, I'm floating above all this, looking down on you, I'm over there *(Pointing at the corner.)* …and now I'm over there! *(Pointing at the ceiling.)*

A Body Not Greatly Changed

Jo J. Adamson

Scene: here and now

Dramatic
Robert: (30s) a man whose wife has committed suicide

> *Gayle's death has left Robert bitter and alienated. Here, he shares a memory of his father.*
>
> *Lights up on Robert coming down the stairs. He's wearing a golf shirt and casual pants. Robert walks over to the stove and pours himself a cup of coffee. He goes over to table, and picks up the paper and looks at it. Robert throws the paper down (his mind wasn't on it anyway) and says to the audience. As if continuing a conversation:*

ROBERT: …It was John Cassavetes, you stupid Son of a Bitch. John Cassavetes played the private dick in "Staccato'." Christ, don't you guys know anything? I'll bet you couldn't even tell me who were "The Untouchables." I'd be willing to bet fifty dollars on that one. Give up? Jerry Paris and Robert Stack were the two Feds who tracked down the Chicago mob. God, I love those gangster shows! Gale would get so mad at me when I watched them. She said the house could burn down and I wouldn't know the difference. I'd *know.* This house is a big damn deal to me. Damn it, I enjoy trivia because it keeps me from thinking too hard. Thinking keeps me awake nights and makes me yell at Gale. *(Robert goes over to stove and gets himself more coffee.)* If this house burned to the ground, I'd go out with it. Gale says she doesn't care for the house. But she's full of it. She begged me to buy it for her. She called it her dream house. Said she wanted to live in it until she died.

My old man used to say that success was making one's age. I earn one-hundred-thousand dollars a year and I'm thirty-five years old. Is that makin' it enough, you old Bastard? Funny, I haven't thought about my dad in years. He died right after I got out of college. The thing I remember most about him was that he used to jingle coins in his pants pockets. Like this... *(Robert comes down stage. He "jingles" the coins in his pocket.)* I loved that sound as a kid. It made me feel secure. My friends called him Old Jingle Pockets. Old Jingle Pockets never bought me a candy bar or soft drink in his life. Never held me, or told me that he was glad that I came into this world. But he sure could make those fuckin' coins sing. *(Robert begins to jingle, with more intensity as he talks.)* I never carried anything but folding bills. It's only been in the last few years, I've begun to collect small change. Lincoln pennies, buffalo nickels, dimes, quarters, dollars. Real dollars, none of that Susan B. two dollar shit. I discovered that twenty dollars in small change makes a good jingle sound... *(Roberts jingles his pockets.)* Can you hear that dad? Listen for Christ's sakes! You've got to listen!

(Lights dim on Robert jingling coins and then out.)

By the Sea, By the Sea, By the Beautiful Sea: "Dawn"

Joe Pintauro

Scene: a beach at dawn, the week of the Perseid meteor showers

Dramatic
Quentin: (30s) a man coping with the loss of his mother

> *Their mother's last wish was that her ashes be scattered over the sea. To this end, Quentin and his sisters have gathered on the beach where their pre-dawn vigil has degenerated into petty sibling bickering. When his sisters condemn his wife for cheating on him, Quentin valiantly defends the woman he loves.*

QUENTIN: Ronnie, remember when we were kids how we used to pray on our knees every night…?

[VERONICA: Q, don't patronize me now…]

QUENTIN: (Overlap.) …For the past ten years I've been falling on my knees before this woman. I'm…I love this woman…more than any thing or person on the face of this earth including you, Mom, anyone…

[VERONICA: Why?]

(Overlap.)

QUENTIN: …because she had the guts to tell me all that you just told me and more that you don't even the fuck know. Which is why she is to me, a million times more attractive than most women could ever aspire to be and believe me, she was beautiful to start out with. But her honesty made her something shining in my life…

[VERONICA: *She betrayed you.*]

QUENTIN: *She shines in my life!* And I fall deeper in love with her every time she falls or fails so there's nothing you can tell me that won't make me *love her more.* There's more to marriage than a souvenir fuck from an old boyfriend. You'd still be married if you realized that.

[PAT: Quentin…]

(Overlap.)

QUENTIN: After you dumped Bob this woman was worried sick about your welfare.

[PAT: Quentin…]

QUENTIN: We'd stay awake in bed at night trying to figure out a way to help you. You sent Bob packing for the same goddamn reason, one little slip and Boom! Overnight, you're the Pope, excommunicating everyone in sight. So, she fucked somebody. Who didn't? There are people fucking people on those planets up there. Horseshoe crabs are fucking in the ocean as we speak. She's good to me. I love her. So do me a favor and find yourself a new Bob. I have my Bob. She's my Bob and I'm hanging on to her. It's dawn, so do what you have to do. I don't want to be here for it. For me it's been over for a long time and I'm going home.

By the Sea, By the Sea, By the Beautiful Sea: "Dusk"

Terrence McNally

Scene: the beach during the week of the Perseid Meteor Shower

Serio-Comic
Willy: (30s) an attractive beachcomber

> *Here, a glib ladies' man chats up a couple of women he's just met on the beach.*

WILLY: I hate people like that, period. I'm Willy. I mean, what's the big deal in talking to one another? Everybody's got some god-damn hidden agenda you're supposed to figure out. Life's too short. You are looking at a man without an agenda. What you see in me is what you get in me. I run about this deep. No, about *this* deep. That doesn't mean I'm shallow. I'm like clear Caribbean water you can see right to the bottom of, even at thirty feet. It just looks like it's shallow, but when you try to dive down to the bottom of it for the sunken treasure, Spanish gold or caskets of jewels you heard or hoped were waiting for you there, you think your lungs are going to explode before you get there. Sometimes you can't do it and you have to shoot back up to the surface for another gulp of air before you can try again. You want my advice? Take it easy. Take a real, real deep breath this time. What's your hurry? I'm worth the effort. I'm that piece of Spanish gold, that pirates' treasure, that king's ransom you've been looking for all your life. I'm right here. A good man is hard to find. I'm a good man. You've found him.

Carpool

Laura Hembree

Scene: a passenger van

Serio-Comic
Carl: (30s) an aggressive member of the carpool

> *When they witness an accident on the way to work, Carl lectures his fellow car-poolers on the importance of paying attention to their environment.*

CARL: It's survival of the fittest, guys. Man turned his head for one second, one second he wasn't looking and BLAM. A little late for work…goes a little faster than usual, some other guy thinking the same thing—BLAM!

[WILLARD: That's what the speed limit's for.]

CARL: It has nothing to do with the speed limit. It has to do with knowing where you are and knowing what you're doing. That guy back there didn't anticipate, see? He's got to anticipate every possibility. Know *who* he is and *where* he is at every point, see?

[WILLARD: I know where I am.]

[GENE: Between exit 7 and exit 8.]

CARL: Those who *know* are more likely to survive.

[WILLARD: Did we pass exit 7 already?]

[GENE: Two cups of coffee, I can survive anything.]

[RAYMOND: …And a couple of Buds.]

CARL: No artificial stimulants. You do it on your own. Now, that guy back there wasn't in tune with the motion of his vehicle, see? He wasn't relying on his basic instinct, or maybe his basic instinct was no good…so he was selected out…*culled* out. He turned his head at the wrong second, moved out of his lane at the wrong time and BLAM—that's it. Nature does not forgive a mistake, see?

Carpool

Laura Hembree

Scene: a passenger van

Dramatic
Willard: (40-50) a man whose wife has been diagnosed with cancer

Here, Willard tells his fellow commuters about the recent changes in his home life.

WILLARD: O.K. *(Pause.)* Her mother's moved in with us, you know. *(No response.)* She's just settled in and taken over. *(No response.)* I guess I can't really complain. *(Pause.)* I'm not sure how the girls like her, but they're getting used to her, I guess…I mean, I guess they're taking this whole thing pretty well…They don't really understand, you know; they just know that their mommy doesn't feel well and that she's losing her hair. That seems particularly disturbing to little Sarah. When Lucille speaks to her, Sarah won't even look at her…but, well, we all think they've been great, really. *(No response.)* And the people at church have been very nice, too. A few Sundays ago the choir donated the altar flowers to Lucille…I think she really appreciated it. I mean, she didn't say anything, but I think she appreciated the gesture. And Pastor John has been mentioning Lucille in his prayers each Sunday, so we're very grateful. I mean, aside from her fatigue, I think she's doing very well. I just tell her we should keep our chin up and count our blessings, you know? That's what I tell her, that we should keep our chin up and count our blessings. *(No response.)* Isn't that right, Dr. Binford?

Carpool

Laura Hembree

Scene: a passenger van

Serio-Comic
Carl: (30s) an aggressive member of the carpool

> *Bitter about his divorce, Carl here cautions his romantically involved friend about the dangers of home redecorating.*

CARL: Picked out the furniture, Gene?

   [GENE: No.]

CARL: Watch out for that designer crap.

   [GENE: Joy's not really into designer…]

CARL: First it'll be the couch, then the curtains, then the pillows…She had to have everything designer.

   [RAYMOND: Who?]

CARL: And I'm still paying for it. That, with the alimony and child support, is about doing me in. We were only married two months and she wanted to re-do the whole apartment. Every night when I came home I had to look at these little pieces of material and tell her if I thought they matched. Finally I told her, "Handle it Sherry, just handle it." Then the carpet came. Have you picked out the carpet?

   [GENE: No.]

CARL: When I came home she was in hysterics. You know why?

   [RAYMOND: What's this got to do with anything?]

CARL: Because the color of the carpet looked different in the store than it did in the apartment. She thought it had too much lavender in it, said it didn't match anything in the room. I said it looked O.K., then she accused me of being color blind; she had me on my fucking knees comparing the curtains to the carpet! Shit, I couldn't stand coming to my own home…and I'm paying for it— that's the killer. I paid for the coffee table and I couldn't even put my feet on it. She made me put paper towels on the damn thing before I put my feet on it.

[WILLARD: Why didn't you just take your shoes off?]

CARL: They were off! I still had to put paper towels up. Then she got pregnant. I told her we couldn't *afford* a kid. But she had it anyway. Women will do that to try and save a marriage, you know. OK, OK, I was willing to give it a shot. I mean it's my seed, right? My seed. My…But it just cried all the time. All it did was cry.

[WILLARD: Some babies cry more than others, Carl.]

CARL: Yeah?

[WILLARD: Yes. Lyla was a crier but Sarah was like a little clam.]

CARL: We were looking for a place anyway, I mean the apartment was getting to feel like a closet—You've seen what happens to rats when they overcrowd them—They become very aggressive and they turn into faggots—that's what happens

[WILLARD: Oh?]

CARL: Yeah, Willard, it's not natural, in case you didn't know.

City Boy in a Cowboy Town

Mark Leiren-Young

Scene: British Columbia

Serio-Comic
Reporter: (20s–30s) a city boy struggling to make sense of his
new home in remote northern B.C.

*Here, the reporter describes a murder case that he covered
for the local paper.*

REPORTER: Typical Cariboo Killing. The first moment I walked into
court in Williams Lake I knew things were different here. The
judge wears cowboy boots. I didn't know this until one of the
Crown Counsels pointed it out to me, but underneath the black
silk robes that represent the traditions of Queen and country, the
provincial court judge wears fancy, leather, cowboy boots. He
isn't a hanging judge or a crazy judge or anything like that but he
is, most definitely, a Cariboo judge. Judge Quentin Ryga. A local
legend. Even if the case was boring it was always interesting to
watch Ryga watching the players. His decisions avoided legal jar-
gon and managed to keep the court process human. And whenever he sentenced someone I felt like he'd agonized over his
decision. That his goal really was rehabilitation—and the good of
society—not vengeance. That's certainly the feeling I got when he
finally sentenced Andrew Milton. Andrew Milton was a twenty-
two-year-old native Indian who was charged with manslaughter
for one of the most scandalous murders in years. At about 8:30
p.m. on a Friday night, a summer night, two years before I arrived
three people were stabbed in downtown Williams Lake. The
three victims were all native. One woman, Pearl Ritchie, a fifty-six-
year old "transient"—people in Williams Lake called them
"Troopers"—died. There were dozens of witnesses but nobody
saw anything. The police conducted an extensive investigation.
They had their suspect. But when they checked the hotels, the
reserves, no one knew anything.

Pearl Ritchie's son wrote a letter to the Tribune. If the victims had been white the murderer would already be in jail. The police were furious with Eric for running the letter. There was a history of two sets of justice in the Cariboo but this case wasn't part of that history. The RCMP knew who had done it, they were after him, they just couldn't find him. Anywhere. Then he broke into a store in Quesnel and they got their man. And they were so desperate to let the community, especially the native community, know the murder had not been forgotten that they actually invited me to the station to tell the story. A story I suspect they would have felt better about if their criminal had seemed…a bit more criminal. The detective who took his statement told me that after the three hour interrogation was over, after a complete confession had been made, Arthur Milton cried and said, *(Softly, take your time.)* "thank you."

I'd often wondered what turns a man into a murderer. In some cases I suspect all it takes is opportunity. In other cases it takes military training and an identifiable enemy. Sometimes it's fear. In Andrew Milton's case it was a couple of joints, a handful of pills and a few bottles of beer. I'd seen criminals in that courtroom who still give me nightmares. There was a trial a week earlier with a pair of thugs who'd held up an elderly couple at rifle point. Both of them grinned as the county court judge sentenced them each to seven years. You could see them calculating exactly how much time they'd serve, how much they'd get off if they played their cards right and who they'd go after as soon as they got out. I don't think I'd ever realized before covering courts that some people actually are truly evil. Andrew Milton had a criminal record too. Nothing dramatic. He got drunk, stole things, hawked them, got drunk again. He'd never hurt anyone—didn't even look like he could. Hell, he was even smaller than me. But that night he went to a party and got really stoned. Somebody insulted him and he pulled a blade. His brother calmed him down and Andrew left the party—to cool off. He headed for the liquor store. Outside the store were three street people—"Troopers."

There were always Troopers outside the liquor store. They

asked Andrew if he had any change. Andrew says he thought they were threatening him, he thought he was being mugged, and he pulled his knife. He swung wildly—stabbing the two men and one woman. Then Andrew ran. He returned to the hotel where he was living and threw out his shirt because it was covered with blood. He threw his knife in a trash bin. And he went into hiding. Williams Lake legend is that he was hidden at various reserves. And maybe that's true. He ran, but he didn't run far. He stayed in the interior of B.C. For two years he and his girlfriend lived in a series of motel rooms and night after night after night Andrew would wake up in a cold sweat after having the same nightmare—nightmares of blood on the ground. Andrew told the court he didn't remember the stabbings. The Crown Counsel described what he'd done, how he'd gone crazy and stabbed three people who just wanted some pocket change. Andrew agreed this must be so. He remembered throwing away the shirt, he remembered throwing away the knife, but he couldn't remember the stabbing. He remembered the blood, but he couldn't remember whose it was. And Andrew Milton sat in the docket and pleaded guilty to a crime he did not remember, but knew in his heart he'd committed.

Friends of the victims watched from the public gallery knowing this man had killed Pearl Ritchie but was not a killer. The Crown Counsel and the public defender both asked for virtually the same sentence, the lowest they could for a murder—five to seven years. They knew Andrew had killed a woman and stabbed two men. They knew he had to go to jail. But no one looked pleased about it. And when Ryga pronounced a sentence of five years he sounded almost ashamed of what he had to do. He called it, "a typical Cariboo killing," which he described as a drunken event usually involving a knife. Ryga wished Andrew well in jail and decreed that psychiatric help should be found. And when the sentence was handed down, Andrew nodded at the judge and said in a voice that was nearly a whisper, "thank you."

The Confession of Many Strangers

Lavonne Mueller

Scene: the Smithsonian Air and Space Museum

Dramatic
Pilot: (60s) the man who flew the *Enola Gay*

> *Here, the man who helped Einstein and Oppenheimer create modern reality relives his famous flight before an audience at the Smithsonian.*

PILOT: *(To the crew of the* Enola Gay.*)* Men, years from now, the citizens of our great country will be watching a movie about what we do today. So…no cussing. No spitting. No scratching. Remain calm but alert. *(He stands and turns to the audience and faces his crew.)* I'll be passing out special goggles to each crew member before take-off. Have them ready to use when I give the order. *(A beat.)* Now, let's go have a good breakfast before we move out. *(To the audience.)* August 5. One a.m. Mess sergeant, Elliott Easterly, had decorated the quonset-mess with cardboard pumpkins. We all took one off the wall for a good luck charm. (A beat.) Two a.m. Our weather planes had already left. Eleven crew members entered the B-29 ahead of me. I was ready to hop on when Dr. Don Young pulled me aside.

(To Dr. Young.) You got something for me, Doc? Twelve cyanide pills? One for each of us? No pain with these, huh? You're right…something goes wrong, I sure as hell don't wanna hit the silk. Guys I've known who got captured by the Japanese were tortured pretty bad. Especially after the fire-bombings in Tokyo. I know…I know…this isn't easy for you. But Doc, I'm planning on success. Didn't we just get a big send-off prayer from the Chaplain? We'll do the job. You'll see.

(To the audience.) On board, I settled into the left seat. Bob Lewis was my co-pilot. We had crew from all around the U.S.— New Mexico, Nevada, Texas, New Jersey, North Carolina, New York, Pennsylvania, Maryland, Michigan, California, and *my* states, Iowa and Illinois.

(Speaking from the captain's seat of the Enola Gay.*)* Crew, synchronize watches. 0230. *(A beat.)* Auxiliary power turned on. *(A beat.)* Electrical system—check. Start up engines. *(A beat.)* All engines go. *(A beat.)* Oil pressure—check. Fuel pressure—check. Brakes set—check. *(A beat.)* Remove the wheel chocks. *(A beat.)* Great Artiste behind us—roger. Ready to taxi out. (He puts both thumbs up.)

(To the audience.) Every take-off is different. It's a crucial time. But now it was important beyond anything I had ever done before. With seven-thousand gallons of gas and a nine-thousand pound atomic bomb, we were loaded well beyond what we should have been. I was determined to remain calm. After all, hadn't I taken off hundreds of times before? I'd just pretend I was with old Earl Ebberly and we were winging our way to Bettendorf, Iowa, to drop candy.

(To the tower.) Redbird six three to North Tinian Tower. Ready for takeoff on Runway Able. *(A beat.)* Cleared for takeoff. Roger. *(To crew.)* Release breaks. *(A beat.)* We're rolling now…two miles of runway and we're just gonna take it slow…we're doing fifty miles an hour…seventy miles an hour…ninety…one-hundred-twenty…end of runway approaching…I'm holding her for ten more miles an hour…I need all the power I can get for lift off. Hold tight…hang on…we're just about there…ahhhhhh…and *up*…at one-hundred-forty miles per hour. Nice and smooth. *(A beat.)* Take off time—0245. Cameras roll.

(To the audience.) Eight minutes airborne, and Parsons began to plug the uranium into the core of "Little Boy." *(A beat.)* Behind us was *Top Secret,* the airplane that would follow us all the way to Iwo Jima in case the *Enola* had some kind of mechanical problem and we needed a spare plane.

(To crew on interphone.) Hey, you guys in isolation, I'm com-

ing back there for a little visit. Yah, I know I gotta crawl thirty feet through a stinking tunnel that's only twenty inches wide. I don't have the belly on me like some of you boozers. I can make it in nothing flat. *(He takes off his shirt and his shoes and socks and crawls back to them. he is in his undershirt, trousers, and barefoot.)* Coming through…coming through. What did I tell you? Slipped right through. *(A beat.)* Nice place you got here. Who's got the hot chocolate? How about hitting me with a cup. Thanks. *(He drinks.)* You guys wanna guess what we have on board? You know it's gotta be important if we were served *real* eggs not powdered eggs for chow. Hey, don't be afraid to speak up. All security's off. This is it. The secret's going to be out pretty damn quick. *(A beat.)* Well, I'll just have to tell you. We're carrying the first Atomic Bomb. Yah! How about that! No kidding. You'll be able to see this bomb from anywhere. Even Paw Paw, Illinois, will see this one. So…what are you guys thinking about right now? Sitting here beside the world's first A-incendiary? *(A beat.)* Buttermilk pancakes! That's what you're thinking about on the most important day of your life? I'll tell you what I'm thinking about. I'm thinking of the word "atom." How it's not going to be a secret or a mystery anymore. One of the scientists— Oppenheimer—told me that a philosopher named Spinoza said a stone falling could think: "I want to fall." I figure that bomb knows it wants to fall, too. *(He crawls back to the captain's seat.)* Altitude fifteen-thousand feet. Wind from the south. *(On interphone.)* Pilot to navigator, keep me posted on any changes in radar wind runs. Over. *(To co-pilot.)* Bob, I think I'll just take a little cat nap. Look after the automatic pilot. And wake me up when we're ready to begin our climb over Iwo Jima.

(To the audience.) I don't think I really slept. At a time like that, your past comes at you in crazy little flashes. The smell of lemon oil furniture polish mom used on holidays. The wallpaper of fading cabbage roses in the parlor. Of course I couldn't get old man Ebberly out of my mind and how he always said I had to "watch the ground." And…I thought about that last time I saw Oppie. Yah, I sometimes called Oppenheimer that like all his sci-

ence buddies. I think he got to like me cause the first thing I said everytime I saw him was—*coffee is coffee.* Not that I ever really understood what the hell that meant. I figure it was like our guys saying "on a wing and a prayer." Anyway, Oppie came to Tinian that day we loaded "Little Boy" on the *Enola.* He watched the whole thing in silence and with a very sad face. His depression shocked me. This was supposed to be the high point of all his hard work. But all he could think about was how the bomb would throw us back into the crude stone age of reason. Because now theory had lost its core. In the final analysis, we should *not* understand. Science is fantasy. For an equation to be true, Oppie reasoned, it was necessary that at least on one level it had to be false. That is why physics was an art. Contradictions. "Little Boy" eliminated what couldn't be solved. There was nothing left for him anymore. *(A beat.)*

Oppenheimer's words wouldn't get out of my head. In some strange way I felt implicated in his depression. But I couldn't understand why. I was doing what he wanted me to do. I was doing what they all wanted me to do…the scientists, Truman…Stimson…Congress…the dead at Pearl if they could speak for themselves. Somehow this wasn't *coffee is coffee.* It might even be some kind of accusation. You could never tell with Oppenheimer. *(A beat.)* It was just beginning to get light. I broke open a little pack of Zinnia seeds Mom gave me and tossed them under my seat for luck. Everything was smooth and steady. When we came to Iwo Jima, I took the controls. Our standby plane swerved away from us and landed. *(A beat.)*

We were now three hours away from our possible targets—either Hiroshima, Kokura or Nagasaki. We were proceeding smoothly, waiting anxiously for instructions from the three weather plane. What would be our target? Oppenheimer said Hiroshima was the best because it had flat terrain that would allow the bomb to "run out." I climbed to thirty-thousand, seven-hundred feet, our bombing altitude. Orders were for a visual drop only. No radar sighting. If we suddenly got bad weather, we were to return to Tinian with Parsons disarming the bomb on the way

31

home. *(A beat.)* People always want to know what I was thinking when I was only moments away from dropping the first A-Bomb. What were my deepest, innermost thoughts? It's hard to remember. In a sense, that man is an illusion to me. He is many illusions. Looking back, which one do I remember? I don't wish to change the thoughts of somebody who is no longer here to defend himself. After all, who I am *now* is not that pilot who has disappeared into history. Yet I know I was probably thinking about Spots and what he said about those horses on his farm that let him rest every two hours…I was also probably thinking about the flights of W W I, and how opposing pilots could lean out of their wood-and-rag planes and fire revolvers at each other. A flying surface was once as human as the flying carpet of the Arabian Nights. Now everything is precision and electronic navigation. When the target was in range, it was procedure at that time for the pilot to remove his hands from the controls and turn the ship over to the bombardier. Technically, I wasn't even at the helm when the pneumatic bomb-bay doors opened and Little Boy dropped. I felt cheated. The only human experience was the explosion and the victims. The days of Earl Ebberly and *The Wilma* when a man hunched down inside the cockpit and let the plane get inside of him were long gone. Now, a pilot simply stepped up and climbs inside the plane. Spots used to talk about his farmer friend, Sig Mosley, who got up one morning and drove his tractor all the way to the coast, then pushed that tractor into the ocean. Said he wanted things to get back to the way they were.

(Into radio.) Straight Flush. Come in. This is *Enola Gay. (A beat.)* Y-3, B-2, C-l. Code received. Roger and out. *(A beat.)* Attention crew. *(A beat.)* The name of our target has just been transmitted from *Straight Flush. (A beat.)* It's…Hiroshima! *(On interphone.)* Pilot to Bombardier. What is the status of "Little Boy?" Bomb is alive. Roger. *(To crew.)* The city is coming into view. Be prepared for Initial Point, fifteen miles east of target. Sighted—eight large ships in the harbor below. No flak visible. *(A beat.)* We are approaching our primary. Secure your goggles on your forehead and prepare to use them at bomb release. Do not

look into the flash. *(A beat.)* All crew, if you agree, please verify by saying after me: "This…is Hiroshima." *(A beat.)* Hiroshima. Check. *(A beat.)* 9:15 and 17 seconds. Hiroshima time: 8:15 and 17 seconds. *(A beat.)* Bombardier, take over the aircraft. *(He holds up his hands away from the controls and moves back in his chair. A beat.)* Bomb-bay doors opening. Little boy…falling. *(After a brief pause, he takes over the controls again.)* Prepare for break-away dive!

(Now stripped to his trousers and sleeveless khaki-undershirt and bare feet, he holds up the chair and turns it sharply to the right in the break-away dive. He says the following monologue while he holds the plane in the break-away dive.) A mushroom foams up at me in a churling mass of spiking mauve gray. Buds of raw green illuminate on every side. The earth's history blooms and exaggerates itself into the atmosphere: Stalks of lamp black and coal tar, stems of sienna, plants of brittle skin gold…shimmering-black leaves…yellow arsenic blossoms. I hear Oppie quoting Montaigne: "And if you have lived one day, you have seen everything. One day is equal to all days. There is no other light, there is no other darkness. The whole disposition of the heavens is the same." Now Montaigne is wrong. It's Oppenheimer's science rotting to the knowable. Today will never be like another day. I have made another light. I have made another darkness. I've changed the Heavens. *(He now begins shaking from the plane's turbulence.)* A fierce boiling red orb, five miles wide, rages towards me at a hundred million degrees. I throw the sun!

Daddy and the Tunnel Rat

Mark Blickley

Scene: Kobi Tan Tan Valley, Vietnam. July 1966

Dramatic
Corporal William Garabente: (20s) a tunnel rat

> *The sole survivor of his unit, Corporal Garabente finds him-*
> *self alone in the jungle of Vietnam facing the dark and gap-*
> *ing maw of a tunnel which he has been ordered to secure.*
> *Here, he encounters the ghost of his father, a G.I. who was*
> *killed in the Battle of the Bulge, and confronts the spirit with*
> *his childhood feelings of grief and abandonment.*

CORPORAL: You know, I never played sports. I spent all my time playing soldier, pretending to be you. Except I never got killed in the end. I always organized these elaborate war games. My uncle bought me this really neat plastic Springfield rifle, like the kind they used in the First World War. It had bolt action loading and everything, but what I loved best was its detachable rubber bayonet. When we'd chose up sides for battle I'd always loan one of the other guys my Springfield and just keep the bayonet 'cause I wanted to be more daring and more special than anyone else in the fight. I wanted to be you. I remember once hiding between two parked cars by the curb, kneeling in dog shit, just so I could ambush the enemy, stab him like I figured you'd done. And now you accuse me of pissing on your grave, and you tell me you never even fought the enemy and here I am stuck in this stinkin' jungle crawling after gooks like the kid kneeling in dog shit, testing myself, trying to cling to the only thing I thought we could share, you fake sonofabitch. And you got the balls to come here and give me shit about going through that tunnel 'cause you're starting not to like the music they play for you at dusk. You see this, Private Garabente. *(He points to his stripes.)* There's only two, Private, but that's twice as much as you have. Christ, you know when I got my promotion it really screwed me up. I kept switching back and forth between thinking how proud you'd be of me and feeling guilty that I outranked you. I thought you were taller than me, tougher than me, but you're just a punk teenager. I'm a man, Private Garabente. I turned twenty-one a few months ago. That's twenty-one years of playing this stupid game. And now I find out there were lies instead of rules.

Easter

Will Scheffer

Scene: a small town in the mid-west

Dramatic
Matthew: (20–30) a man whose wife has been driven to madness by the death of their child

> *Matthew and Wilma have been on the run since the death of their baby. Wilma's suppressed grief and rage have caused her to act out by burning down churches. Here, Matthew finally tells his story to a strange old man who is constantly tuned-in to television…with or without a TV set.*

MATTHEW: It was about seven years ago. *(Long pause.)* We were livin' in Taloga. Things were good for us. Not great. But we were happy. I wasn't a football star, but I had a good little construction business. And most of the time, we did alright. Wilma worked part time as a secretary at the church. Never went to services or nothin'. It was just her job. We had a simple life. Nice. Sometimes for fun, we'd play poker with friends or go line dancin'. We'd wanted a baby for awhile but it took us some time to get pregnant. The day Wilma told me we were gonna have a baby, I was—God—I was so happy. I went right out and got drunk, came home late that night with a big shiny red bicycle. I knew it was gonna be a boy. Wilma laughed at me. Said I shouldn't count my chickens. But I didn't care what she said. I was so happy I went outside in the moonlight and threw the football back and forth to myself…

[ZADDOCK: Go on, go on, go on.]

MATTHEW: Well, at this time we were livin' in a small house, way outside of town, and in those next few months my business started slackin' off a bit, and I was feelin' a little upset about it and all. The bills were piling up and I guess I was drinkin' a little too much. My car wasn't in good shape and Wilma kept tellin' me to take it in to the garage, but I didn't have the money. One day they turned off the telephone. I got so pissed off I put my hand through the window. Me and Wilma had a little fight and I went out to a bar. When I come back she was washin' out her hair in the sink. It was about a month before the baby was due. She didn't even look at me when I came in, just kept washin' her hair. I was about to say I was sorry when all of a sudden she turned. She screamed out a little. She was holdin' her belly. I asked her what was wrong—and she started to say somethin', but before the words could come she screamed out again and a splash of blood hit the linoleum underneath her like paint. I ran to her and she kind of fell into my arms. I didn't know what to do. I lay her down on the floor and wrapped her in a blanket.

I ran out to start up the car, but it wouldn't turn over. From inside the house I heard her screamin'. I ran back inside and when I got there I saw two little legs comin' out of her. Two little legs and feet and they were kickin'…movin'…blood everywhere. Oh my God I think I'm gonna be sick… *(Matthew rolls down the window to take some air. The light from a neon sign flashes on and off, pink on his face.)* I carried her to the hospital. Carried her in my arms those two miles. For awhile the legs kept kickin' but by the time I got her there…they had stopped. Doctor said she was lucky to be alive. Said it was the worst birth he'd ever seen. Next day when Wilma woke up, they brought the little dead thing into the room and let her hold it in her arms. She called it Herman. She wouldn't stop talkin' to it. All that day she wouldn't let it go. And when I finally got it away from her she screamed and screamed at me. Hospital let me take it home—you know—to bury it. They gave it to me in a plastic bag. It was so…little. And later that day, when I was alone, I held it too. I held it in my arms. *(Pause.)* I tried to—to help her forget, to make it be like we were. But somewhere—I think she stopped lovin' me. *(Pause.)* That's the whole of it. The whole story. You want it? You can have it.

37

Epic Poetry

James Bosley

Scene: the Amazon Saloon. A mythical time in the NY tri-state area

Serio-Comic
Ulysses: (40s–50s) a lost hero

> *Here, a modern incarnation of a familiar wanderer tells his son, Jason, about the importance of taking care of one's mother.*

ULYSSES: Well, my mother was a great woman. She worked very hard, cleaning, cooking, sewing. She loved me, she loved my father—which in itself was no easy chore. And she tried to teach me to be good. But I didn't want to be good. I wanted to fight and drink beer and hang around with other bad boys. And bad girls.

[JASON: Why?]

ULYSSES: I guess I thought being bad was more fun, and that being good was just for nice ladies like my Mom. But I couldn't be bad around her because that would make her cry. And that would make my father really mad. So I ran away from home to find out if there was more to life than just being good all the time.

[JASON: Did you find out?]

ULYSSES: You know, I got so involved in the fighting, the drinking beer and so on, that I never stopped to think about it. I went from war to war and bed to bed, not wondering what's right, what's wrong, just wondering—what's next.

[JASON: So why do you have her name on your arm?]

ULYSSES: Oh, I was off somewhere and heard she was dying. I raced back to see her—to tell her—what, I'm sorry? But I was too late. Got back in time for the funeral. Well there was a lot of people there—some people I knew, but all these strangers were there too. And these strangers kept coming up to me and telling me what a wonderful woman my mother was. Turns out these were people that she'd helped over the years. People who were sick, or didn't have a place to live, she'd take them in. Feed them. And if anybody asked her why she was doing all this for people she didn't even know she would say to them, "My son is out there somewhere and who knows, maybe he's sick or needs a place to stay. I only hope that someone does for him what I'm doing for someone else's son. When I heard that—

[JASON: What?]

ULYSSES: Let me see if I can explain it to you. I was sad that she died. And I was mad at myself for never appreciating her. But at the same time I was happy for knowing that while I was off doing the dumb things I was doing, she never stopped loving me. So I was sad and mad and happy all together. And I just busted out crying.

[JASON: You cried?]

ULYSSES: That was the only time. And that's when I got this tattoo, so I'd never forget her. *(Ulysses towels his face. Puts on his shirt.)* So let that be a lesson to you. No matter how bad you are, your mother will always love you. And if I'm not around, you be good and mind her, and take care of her. Because she deserves it. You got that?

Feathers in the Dust

Richard Lay

Scene: a train

Serio-Comic
Bod: (30s) a man searching for a lost love

> *Bod rides trains in search of a woman with whom he has
> fallen in love. Here, he tells his story.*

BOD: She was in a wheelchair.

[POKE: (Excited.) What happened?]

BOD: I was on one of my usual wrong trains and while I was thinking…the train stopped at a station I had never been to before. I
looked through the grimy window and saw this young woman
with red hair. She was wearing a white dress and facing the train.
A big black man was with her with his hands on the wheelchair
handles…On instinct I winked at her…and to my surprise she
winked back and gave me a wonderful smile. Then the train
moved off and she waved to me… So to tell you the truth, the
honest version of the truth…ONE of the reasons I travel on wrong
trains is to try and see her again…And day after day I fail. I don't
know who she is, where she's from, or what's wrong with her. I
AM IN LOVE…if I was quiet at that last stop it was because I was
looking for HER. Try being in love With someone you don't know.

[POKE: What's her name? What's your best guess?]

BOD: I thought that just for my thoughts I would call her Miss
Chair. For a first name I thought Wheel has a sort of ring about
it…I love her, I can't have her, I don't know who she is…I only
have the memory of the smile. She looked so contented. If she
didn't like me calling her Miss Wheel Chair in the absence of a
real name…if I found her…I would, quite naturally, switch to her
given name.

The Golem

Andrew C. Ordover

Scene: the Jewish Quarter of Prague, Spring, 1592

Dramatic
Judah ben Bezalel Loew: (50) chief Rabbi of Prague

> *Here, the Rabbi tells the tale of how he first met and fell in love with his beloved late wife, Perl.*

LOEW: You know. when I look at you standing there, it's like I'm seeing *her* again—like I'm seeing her for the very first time, that day in Poland. My beloved Perl…

 [GITTL: Tell us how you met her, Rabbi. I've never heard the story.]

LOEW: Oh. Well. It's a story. You see, her father was a baker, but after we got engaged, he lost all his money. He wrote to release me from the contract, but I wouldn't hear of it. Of course. I had never met Perl, only heard about her, so I left the yeshiva to see this woman who was maybe to be mine and maybe not.

 [GITTL: This is so romantic…]

LOEW: Now Perl was working in the bakery when I arrived, but before I could introduce myself, a soldier rode by and speared a loaf of bread. She caught the horse by the bridle and nearly tore the man off his saddle. So the soldier pulled his sword, and my Perl fell to her knees: "Please, my father has lost all his money. All I ask is that you pay for what you took." And I'm thinking, what to do, what to do? But the soldier sees the look in her eyes. and he stops. He gives her a little bundle and says, "here, you hold this for me. If I don't come back with the price of the bread, it's yours to keep." And he rides off.

 [ISAAC: Did he come back?]

LOEW: She knew he wouldn't. So she opened up the bundle, and what do you think she found? Enough gold to pay her father's debts. She sat on the ground, holding the gold pieces, and she started to cry. And I kneeled beside her, and said, "I have never seen such courage before. Never, outside the storybooks. I would marry you if there was nothing in that bundle but straw."

Good Guy's Wear Yellow

Daphne R. Hull

Scene: here and now

Dramatic
Horatio: (30s) a genetic engineer suffering from an attack of conscience

> *Although Horatio has devoted his professional career to improving the genetic structure of humanity, he has recently come to respect the importance of serendipity as he here describes.*

HORATIO: *(Reads what he has written, after typing briefly.)* To whom it may concern. Hmmm. That may be a little too formal. Let's think about this a second. *(Gets up and paces; loftily, Shakespearean.)* To whom it may concern. *(Pauses, sits.)* I guess that will simply have to do. I wouldn't have a clue who to address it to specifically, if I were going to be specific. It stands as written: To whom it may concern. *(Pauses with fingers poised over keys, types again, stops.)* If you are reading this, and I assume you are, otherwise I would be wasting my breath—or keystrokes—if you are reading this, I assume you are searching for an explanation. *(Types, stops.)* I don't feel like I owe any explanations, or owe anyone a thing, generally, but for the purposes of satiating the curious, and admittedly, satiating myself to some extent, I shall attempt to provide one. *(Pause, sips, types.)* On second thought… *(Pause.)* there is no explanation for what I have done. What I can offer is a series of observations and remarks, open for you to interpret your own explanation, your own answer to sew it up, your own fire in the hole. That will have to suffice. *(Runs hand through hair, sips water.)* I was recognized with a cash bonus from work last week. *(Types.)* I was also assured a promotion, next in line after the assistant to the deputy V.P. of the

43

Genetic Engineering Department retires in the fall. My supervisor slapped me on the back and said, *(Puffy southern drawl.)* "Not bad for the new kid on the block, eh?" Not bad at all. New kid. I've been the new kid for six years. *(Types, reads.)* It is customary for any guy who has good fortune to treat the department to a round of beers after work. I guess this was expected of me as well. What is expected is not always received. The other engineers were putting their coats and hats on as slowly as possible, and some were sort of hanging by the door. I guess they were waiting for me to ask. I didn't. I pretended not to see. *(Pause, types, reads.)* I came straight back to my apartment. I thought little of it, until the next day, when I began to get the feeling that I had suddenly become rather unpopular. It is not as if I previously could have been considered popular, but now I was most definitely and unequivocally unpopular. I had moved from a neutral status to one of the extremes. I seem to have broken an unwritten rule of the work force camaraderie: *(Exaggerated fire and brimstone.)* SHARE THY SUCCESS WITH THY BROTHERS, or THOU SHALT FEEL THE WRATH. *(Beat, thoughtful.)* Perhaps someone should write down all of the unwritten rules. *(Gets up, paces, stands and thinks while looking at a painting, returns to desk and types.)* In my profession, I, and others like me, delve into genetic possibilities every day. Upon gaining some expertise, and testing for results, these possibilities become certainties, and the randomness, along with the anticipation of discovery, dissipates. *(Slightly sarcastic.)* The previous thrill of raw, lascivious searches for true answers fades into a sophisticated defense mechanism, where one must no longer prove for the sake of proving, but instead must prove oneself to be absolutely correct in one's hypotheses and calculations. Breakthroughs have given over to accuracy wrapped up tight in a pretty box. *(Sips, types, reads excitedly.)* In the lab, I can direct my computer to reconstruct and rearrange genes and DNA to create any type of person I—or my boss—wants to create. I am Bernstein, I am Zinman of the gene pool, conducting, pounding out a chromosomal coda, repeated over and over with subtle differences every time it is played. I can create clones, a slew of clones, if I want to. Perhaps—perhaps if Hitler had access to this knowledge, he would have approached genocide from a different angle, one more suited to the tastes of the masses. Perhaps he would have been gracious and simply sterilized all the Jews, let them die off, and created his superior race with a keyboard. *(Yiddish singsong.)* Much less messy. *(Normal voice.)* He may have been far too interested in flexing his muscles to take such a cerebral approach, but I wouldn't be here if he hadn't been so sloppy. His human capacity for error gave many of us life, directly or indirectly. And as for Hitler's successor? *(Quiet, then types, reads.)* The Union of Concerned Scientists are very concerned, as are the liberal media and the bible thumpers. Strange bedfellows. Anyway. I digress. *(Pause.)* It took two or three years before I became weary of all this certainty. I knew what to expect when I awoke, when I arrived at work, when I came, and when I slept. No surprises. No plot twists. No nothing. About two months ago, after a long day of designing large quantities of various necessary people, I left work and found my car wouldn't start. *(Smiles.)* It was Fate, throwing a wrench into my routine and greeting me with a beckoning hand. I walked back to my apartment. On the way, I passed an art supply store. I stared in the window, and started to walk on several times, but kept stopping and turning back. Finally, I resigned myself to my own curiosity and ventured in. I emerged, hours later, with bags and armfuls of materials I knew nothing about, most of which I had not the foggiest idea how to use. *(Smiles.)* I bought them all under the advice of a smiling salesgirl with crooked teeth and an unusual nose. As I checked out, I found myself wondering how to adjust her DNA to fix those little imperfections. *(Pause.)* I lugged everything into my apartment, spread it out on the floor, and stared at it all for a long time. Weeks. I decided eventually that since I had invested the money into these things, I might as well see what they could do. *(Very expressive at this point; more use of hands and boyish enthusiasm. He is describing his transformation and rebirth.)* I slashed and attacked the canvas like an amateur—which is exactly what I am. *(Types, reads.)* I let the paint fall wherever it wanted to, or wherever I felt like having it fall. Finally, I had something requiring no blueprint, something never quite complete or incomplete, something never quite perfect—random splashes holding little meaning except to me. *(Pause, stands, gestures to paintings.)* That's what I did the day I received my cash bonus, instead of taking everyone out. I came home to paint. I never thought to tell them that I was going home to paint, it didn't occur to me to explain away my silent declinations. If I had, they probably would not have understood. I had never informed anyone of my activities after work. *(Pause, types, reads.)* During the last few days of tepid relations, once I established their source, I realized that even had I known the outcome, the consequence, I would have done the same thing that evening. *(Pause, excited again.)* I have caught myself actually daydreaming at the terminal. For how long, I don't know, I just come out of it and I've been there. Through these dreams, I have concluded there is a definite and critical need for randomness and uncertainty. *(To himself, exclaims.)* Something that surprises! *(Types, then reads.)* Yesterday, on my way home from work, again forgoing machinery for manpower, a car barreled through a mud puddle and I was thoroughly soaked. As I peeled my dripping socks from my feet, I thought, how random can you get? What is the probability that I, not anyone else, would be standing on that particular street corner at that particular moment when that particular car drove through that pothole and that the pothole would be filled with rainwater? So. The pothole brings me to today. *(Sips, types, reads silently, then paces, paper in hand.)* Today, I went to work, same as always, and carried out my routine duties. *(Slow smile.)* With a small plot twist. I decided to exert a high locus of control over a system possessing a incredible amount of control over all of us. *(Pause, pleased.)* I erased everything. Everything. All my programs, all my data, all my notes, everything. Wiped the drive clean. I came home and burned the backup tapes. Everything. The key to success has been swallowed. *(Walks to desk, sips water.)* The russian roulette of pure human reproduction will have to suffice, at least for a while, until the others retrace my steps and play catch-up. I took the rest of my cash bonus and made preparations to erase myself as well. *(Opens desk drawer and takes out a gun; sips water, holds up gun and spins cylinder.)* To keep me from changing my mind.

(Puts gun to temple; lights go out as there is a loud gunshot.)

The Government Inspector

Nikolai Gogol

New Adaptation by Philip Goulding

Scene: a provincial town

Serio-Comic
Joseph: (20s) disgruntled valet to a minor government clerk

> *Joseph's employer is a traveling clerk whose extravagant habits have depleted their funds. Stranded in a small town in the country, Joseph here grouses as he polishes his master's shoes.*

JOSEPH: I'm so hungry. If I don't get some food inside me soon my stomach will start eating itself. And God knows where that will end. Heart, lungs, liver. I may end up disappearing altogether. Not that *he* would notice. I'm beginning to think we'll never make it home. Two months now in the middle of nowhere. What money we had—squandered. He always has to over-reach himself. "Book the best room Joseph, order the finest food. Nothing but the best—that must be our motto!" All for the sake of appearance. And what has he got to show off about? He's just a clerk. Just a glorified pen-pusher. Not even glorified now I come to think of it. But there are always friends to be made, cards to be played. And without fail he manages to lose. *(Pause.)* Oh I suppose there are arguments for country living The slower pace. And the peasant girls. But no, it's not for me. I'm the city sort, I can't adapt. Of course you need money in your pocket. But given that you can't beat it. The theatre! The dance halls! The races! A bit of refinement, that's what it comes down to. *(Spits on the shoe.)* It's "Good day sir" and "How do you do." Not "What cheer mush" and "Marnin' you." And you're never alone in the city. There's always someone with something interesting to say. It's…civilized is what it is. You can walk in the park and take in

48

the scenery. Parlour-maids. Housemaids. Nursemaids Ladies-maids. Lovely! And everybody treats you like a gent. You feel a bit tired, you hop in a cab. And if you don't feel like paying you just pull up somewhere and tell them to wait. Hop out and then leg it down an alley. They're none the wiser. It doesn't hurt. But him…His trouble is he could never handle money. His old man sends a bundle and he just fritters it away. Takes cabs everywhere, and pays! Theatre tickets every day. He's never been one for work. he'd rather gamble or pose. And he's useless at both. *(Pause.)* So here we are. No more food till we've paid the bill. If I don't eat soon I'm done for. *(Doubles up.)* I think my kidneys are under siege.

The Government Inspector

Nikolai Gogol

New Adaptation by Philip Goulding

Scene: a provincial town

Serio-Comic
Petty: (20s) a foolish young clerk

> *When Petty is mistaken for a Government Inspector, the people of the small town roll out the red carpet for the young impostor. Enjoying his unexpected status Petty here babbles inanely to an attractive young woman.*

PETTY: Literature's my life-blood, nothing less! I host the best-respected salon in the city. Everybody knows it. Strangers point as they pass "That's John Petty's place" they cry. I say! If you're ever in the city, I trust you'll all honour me with your presence. My balls are the talk of the town.

[ANNA: How magnificent they must be.]

PETTY: Taste, of course, is the key. As the centre-piece, a huge water melon. I won't bore you with the cost of such a thing. A thousand pounds at least. The soup I have imported, directly from Par-ee. In special tureens. You lift the lids and…! That aroma! It'd bring you to your knees. *(Finds himself holding Anna's knee. Hauls her up and spins her round.)* We dance all night and when we're tired of that… *(Discards her.)* …there's always whist. It's a pretty exclusive club, of course. The Foreign Minister himself, the French Ambassador, the German Foreign Minister, and me. It's quite exhausting keeping up. Though languages are my special-ity. Then by the time I get home I can hardly make it up those four flights of stairs to my flat. My major-domo stumbles out of the kitchen and I cry… *(Seeks inspiration. His gaze finds Anna.)* "Sidebottom! Quick as you can! Take my coat, there's a good man!" *(Pause.)* Wait a minute. What am I saying? What absolute

50

nonsense. *(Beat.)* Forgive me…I'm forgetting. *(Beat.)* Of course. I live on the *first* floor. *(All breathe a sigh of relief.)* Ah, but if you could peep into that fabulous reception room early in the morning, before I'm even up and out. Princes and Counts, buzzing about. Like bees round a honey pot. Moths to a flame. Sometimes even the Prime Minister drops by. *(All leap to attention.)* And my letters of course, come addressed "To His Excellency." I remember once I had to take charge of the entire department. The Director had disappeared for some reason, mysteriously, no-one knew where. There was a great deal of talk as to who should take his place. Some of our great Generals tried to fill the post, but it was hopeless, one after another they had to admit defeat. So the task naturally fell to me. A complete surprise of course. I went out onto my balcony one morning to find crowds of messengers in the street. Thirty-five…thousand at least! A cry went up—"Your country needs you!" At first I thought it politer to refuse. Out of modesty. But come lunchtime public order was threatened, so I had to reluctantly concede. After all, if it reached the ears of Her Majesty heaven knows what the outcome might be. "But I must warn you" I said, "There'll be changes at every level! No stone will remain unturned in my search for inefficiency and corruption!" That stirred them up I can tell you. Like an earthquake it was. Every man among them shook. Like leaves. *(All shake.)* "There is a new power in the land!" I told them. "I am ubiquitous. I am omnipotent! I've an open invitation to the Palace! I am everywhere! And what's more…tomorrow…I shall be…Field-Marshal!"

Hazing the Monkey

Marcus A. Hennessy

Scene: here and now

Dramatic
Roger: (20s) a disillusioned young man

> *Roger walked away from life as a musician in a bar band to marry Sally and settle down. His new job has taken him well inside the corporate milieu, where he is driven crazy by the new generation of business-speak mumbo jumbo. When his CEO, Mrs. Kaiser, has a heart attack at the office, Roger finally explodes as his co-workers debate the correct office protocol to handle the emergency.*

ROGER: Oh no you don't! I'm not falling for this shit anymore! What do you call this? WHAT?! The...the Resurrection Module? The Raise-the-Dead-CEO Module?...

[MS. FINCH: Roger, this is not a module! This is reality! Mrs. Kaiser is obviously...]

ROGER: Is obviously playing possum. Isn't that right, Mrs. Kaiser? Or maybe it's not even Mrs. Kaiser at all. Maybe it's some actor, straight from Hollywood, with a line from "Murder She Wrote"! *(Roger goes over, leans close to Mrs. Kaiser's head and blows a big razzberry.)*

[REV. DARWIN: Show some respect, young man!]

ROGER: Respect for what? See, I figured it all out... The purpose of this module is to find out how Roger handles a stressful situation where it looks like somebody just up and dies on him...Does he panic, lose his cool, or does he throw her down on the ground and bust his best CPR moves until you yell "Time!", or you stop doubting him, or you shove your tits in his face? Or, do I just wave my hand over her and say, "Rise, woman, for by the power of God in me, you are healed!" Well I don't have that power, all right? I am not some kind of superman. I may not even be that good as a man! I tried...I tried to be good... But for who? Who was I good for? Mrs. Kaiser? You? Sally?

(Rev. Darwin kneels in front of the desk and begins to pray. Roger moves towards the door.)

ROGER: Sure, go ahead and pray, Reverend. Pray that I don't go out to my car, get a gun and come back to fuck all the women and kill all the managers!

[MR. DIKTER: You're joking, aren't you?]

ROGER: *(At Mrs. Kaiser.)* Okay, you can get up now, Mrs. Kaiser. Roger has left the building!

Icarus

Edwin Sanchez

Scene: a beach house

Dramatic
Beau: (20–30) a man hiding from the past and from himself

> *Beau wears a mask which he claims hides a face that has been horribly disfigured in a car crash. When he meets Altagracia, a remarkable woman who was born with a horribly ugly face, Beau is transformed by her strength and inner beauty, making it possible for him to finally reveal his own, perfect, face and confess his sad story.*

BEAU: I had this plan of going to Hollywood to be discovered. So me and my brother stole the family car and took off. Hey, with my looks how could I miss? We were driving on some back road in Texas and I'm massaging Phillip's neck when this jeep pulls up alongside us and I hear someone yell "Faggot!" and this beer bottle comes flying at us. Phillip floors it, turns off the lights and tries to lose them. All the time I'm thinking, "Wait a second, we're not gay. We're brothers. This is a mistake." They force us off the road and drag us out of the car. They shine a flashlight in Phillip's face, then mine. And like an idiot I smile. Hey, my smile was always my secret weapon. Somebody punches me in the stomach and Phillip screams to leave me alone. So they hold me down and beat him. Take out a baseball bat and beat him. They make me kiss the bat with my brother's blood. And I do. Cause I was afraid. Cause I was,…am a coward. See, that's something you would never have done. You would have let them kill you. You would have found a way to save your brother. I see Phillip die and when they're done with him the gang leader takes my face in his hands. So gently. "Don't cry, you can do better, you're so beautiful," then he spits in my face and they scatter leaving me to me. My brother lies dead, while you promise yours the sun. See how your eyes fooled you? See how I'm even less than you thought I was?

In Search of the Red River Dog

Sandra Perlman

Scene: a trailer home in Deerfield, OH. August, 1978

Dramatic
Denny: (20s) a young man ruined by tragedy

> *Denny has lost his job, his child and his wife's love in a very short amount of time. Frustrated and ultimately enraged by his wife's refusal of physical closeness, he savagely rapes her. As she prepares to leave him, he begs her to stay.*

DENNY: I wish I may…I wish I might! Paulette I wish that I may make you stay with me tonight. Make it all so right again, please baby…

[Paulette drops the suitcase.]

DENNY: If you just stay, stay here with me tonight, baby, oh, God, Paulette, please, just stay here with me tonight under the stars…the constellations, the ones you love. I swear I'll learn the name of every one of them for you. I'll learn them and we'll wish on them together every night just like you always wanted. Together. And I'll even help you hang those sheets right out here in the moonlight to dry. If you stay. You'll see, it will be different. I promise, just one more chance and—

[Paulette picks up the suitcase without looking at him and starts to walk.]

DENNY: You gotta believe in me, you gotta give me one more chance so I can show you it's gonna be different. If you just believe—

(Denny grabs her and Paulette pulls away.)

DENNY: I won't touch you, not if you don't want me to Paulette. I promise. I won't touch you anywhere you don't want me to touch you unless you tell me you want me…until you beg me. I'll change, you'll see that, I won't be the man you hate right now, no, I won't ever be that man again, not if you stay. I'll change and you'll love me like you used to when we first met. You remember that, don't you honey? Out behind the football field, me just standing there in my uniform with my foot all wrapped up all lonely and waiting for you. You'll see. You'll love me just like you used to. I'll get a good job with big money and we'll sell this old sardine can and move wherever you want to go. You can go to school or work or just plant the biggest garden in all Ohio. Anything you want baby. I promise. I'll treat you like a Queen. You'll see. I'll be anything you want if you just don't leave me now.

[Paulette pauses and then walks off.]

DENNY: PAULETTE! If you leave me now you can never come back. I swear to you if you keep walking down that road now it is over between us forever. Do you hear that? Forever. I'm through with you forever and you can never come back here. Do you hear what I'm saying to you Paulette! If you keep on walking you can never come back home again. *(Pause.)* Paulette! Don't you hear me?

Jack Flew

David Ippolito

Scene: NYC

Dramatic
Jon: (70s) a widower who has just witnessed a miracle

> *While walking near the 59th Street Bridge, Jon and others watched in amazement as a homeless man flew. Here, lonely Jon describes the remarkable event to his dead wife.*

> *(Lights up on Jon, alone in his apartment. He is boiling water to make himself a cup of instant coffee. Standing over the stove, he lifts the kettle from the flame.)*

JON: A watched pot… *(He puts the kettle back down, reaches for the jar of instant coffee, and prepares the cup. He speaks as he does this. His movements are slow, but deliberate.)* A watched pot…a watched pot. *(He picks up the kettle and puts it back down again. He begins to slowly walk backward, almost in a slow motion stagger, and backs into his favorite chair. He slumps back.)* Oh, Miriam. What am I going to do? *(Pause.)* Hmmm? My day? *(Pause.)* Well, Miriam, I had a typically nice day, all in all. *(Pause.)* I went to the park this morning. That pain in the butt woman was there with her dog, the woman who never pooper scoops. Almost said something to her, but…you know…Stopped in on Art. He's doing much better, although *he* says his doctors don't think so. But I told him *I* think he is. There's a little light in his eyes and the color is back in his face. That must be good. His eyes are a lot clearer than the last time I saw him. Who knows? Maybe they just changed his medication. But I think he's doing much better. We had a nice visit. Didn't stay too long. A nice visit. Then I went over to the social security office to clear up that matter. They're surprisingly nice people over there for government workers. Got everything taken care of, finally. On the way back, I saw a homeless man flying...then I stopped at the market. Ooh! Produce is so expensive this year. Early frost or something. But, I picked up some vegetables. Oh, some eggplant and some of that bread you and I like so much, and came home. *(He slaps his thighs and rises to his feet.)* Coffee. I know. I know. Caffeine. But it hasn't killed me, yet. *(He pours the hot water into the cup he has prepared.)* Instant. Oh, well. *(He stirs the coffee.)* Saw a homeless man fly. Did I mention that? *(He stops stirring. Pause. He abruptly sits back down in his chair.)* Oh, Miriam. Am I losing my mind? *(He sips his coffee, but it's too hot to drink.)* No. There were others. They saw it. He flew. The man flew, Miriam. You should have seen it. Just up...up...so gently and around. The most remarkable...you should have seen it. *(Pause.)* Perhaps you did. *(He starts to sip, but thinks better of it.)* What to do. *(Pause. He raises his cup to his lips again, doesn't drink, and lowers it.)* Miriam, I'm old. I'm an old man. When did that happen? When did we get old? *(He starts to get out of the chair but stops suddenly.)* Miriam, I saw a homeless man fly today... *(Pause.)* What am I supposed to do? You would know. What could it mean? What could have happened to make...there's got to be some explanation. Must be...some sensible, sane, rational explanation. *(Pause.)* All the years, a lifetime, really, saying I believe certain things...saying *we* believed things, and all the time in the back of our minds... *(Shakes his head.)* doubting...wondering...not *really* being able to believe half of what we say at all. *(He sips his coffee.)* Well, here it is. Heh. *(He sips coffee.)* One would think something like this would instantly verify everything I ever wondered about the supernatural or... *(Pause.)* Heh! Well, it doesn't! *(Pause.)* It's just too fantastic. *(He sips.)* Perhaps this means the things that we can't see...are, in truth, the most real... *(Shakes his head.)* Maybe it means nothing. *(He puts his coffee down.)* But...perhaps it means that you really *can* hear me, Miriam. And maybe I haven't been...talking to the air...all these years since you left. *(He looks up and around, suddenly overcome with the thought. He slips out of the chair and slumps to the floor.)* Oh, Miriam. I miss you so much. I miss you, Miriam. God, why couldn't

59

I have gone first. I'm not wishing this unbearable loneliness on you, mind you, but I think you could have handled it better than I. And now, all of the sudden, it's much worse. Suddenly, I'm aching to hold you, Miriam. To look at your sweet face and ask you what I'm supposed to do. I thought the ache of missing you would lessen with time. What a fool. How could I be so foolish. God, I wish you were here. *(Pause.)* Can you hear me? Please, what am I supposed to do? You would know. You would make it all right. *(He composes himself a little.)* Who knows, this might even be a little adventure if you were here with me. If you were here to share it with me. We could explore this together. *(Breathes deeply.)* What happened back there, today? *(Tries to pull himself together.)* I know. I know. I've lived long enough. You'd think nothing would surprise me! But, gimme a break! This is a curve ball Ted Williams couldn't see coming! *(He hefts himself back up into the chair.)* Miracles! They're not supposed to happen anymore! Everyone knows that! And if God wants to pull off a miracle, he should be a little more subtle! Consider that an old man might be in the vicinity…might have a heart attack and drop dead! He flew right up off the ground, Miriam! Right in front of me! Nothing very subtle about that, I'll tell you! *(Pause.)* What to do. *(He stands.)* Miracle-schmeeracle! I *am* losing my mind…it's OK…I'm old. Ooooh. But there were others. They all saw it, too. I know they did. That young woman started crying. That was *probably* the most appropriate response! Ha! *(Pause.)* But, no one said a word. We all just went our separate ways. How curious! "That man just flew. Yes, well, goodbye. Have a nice day." What were we thinking? *(Pause.)* We *weren't* thinking. We were too busy soiling ourselves. *(Pause.)* Understandable. Hmph. *(Sits back down slowly.)* But, do you know, Miriam? Right at this moment, I'm not at all frightened. I wasn't even really frightened as it was happening. Just…amazed. No. Astonished, really. I am astonished at what happened and the way we all reacted. Absolutely astonished… *(Pause.)* And… *(He slumps back in the chair.)* …very alone. *(He closes his eyes.)* Oh, I miss you.

(He breathes deeply. There is a long silence. Lights out.)

L'Eboueur Sleeps Tonight
(For worlds are destroyed every day.)
Jerome D. Hairston

Scene: here and now

Dramatic
Dookie: (30s) a small-time hit man in love

> *Years of living a violent life have left an indelible mark on Dookie, who has fallen for Marilyn, a prostitute. Here, he makes an awkward proposal of marriage.*

> [MARILYN: So, I'm supposed to trust my life to a murderer. Some ruthless monster, cold blooded killer.]

DOOKIE: You really tryin' to kill the mood here, ain't you? You could at least give me the benefit of the doubt. I'm tryin' to make some poetry out of the situation.

> [MARILYN: Poetic? Is that what you call it?. You killed a pimp and got stuck with a whore. That's not poetry. That's bad luck.]

DOOKIE: Not the way I see it. Looks to me you spent most your life flirting with a razor blade in hopes death will come sweep you off your feet. Well, here I am. That ain't bad luck. That's fate.

> [MARILYN: Sweep me off my feet, huh? I'm havin' a hard time finding the romance in all this. Cereal and a cheap ass ring that don't even fit?]

DOOKIE: How you know it don't fit?

> [MARILYN: Get real, Dookie. It's made for children.]

DOOKIE: *(Kneels with ring in hand.)* Well, it's supposed to be one size fits all. Bendable plastic. To fit your needs. *(Placing the ring on her finger.)* See, it didn't break. Things can be what you ain't never expect. Look, I might not be no Prince Charming. But I'm here. I'm just tryin' to do somethin' with that. That ain't criminal, is it?

[MARILYN: Yes, it is. You don't ask somebody like me, some-thing like this. It's not fair. Anybody else wouldn't even listen. But who do you ask? Some cum stained cooze, who ain't got no reason to tell you no. Who are you supposed to be? Mr. Diamond eyes? Knight in shiny polyester? You think you're that much of a prize?]

DOOKIE: I ain't a prize. Take a gander. I'm wrecked. Eighteen hours I've been pacin' around this joint. I've come across the most dan-gerous pistol packin' punks in this piss smellin' city, and not shud-derin' twice about the consequences. But last night, I find myself a shakin' son of a bitch thinkin' about, about…

[MARILYN: About what?]

DOOKIE: You. Me. This life. *(Pause.)* I'm pointin' the barrel right between a man's eyes. I can see his whole world fallen to pieces. Every thing he know and love in this world, eradicated next two seconds. What's it mean to me? Worlds are destroyed just about everyday far as I'm concerned. But I need to know what it's like. To have a world to lose. So I can bring a little something to the table. Somethin' that'll help m, I don't know, grow? Is that it? I need to grow or somethin'? I'll make it worth your while. Whatever you want in exchange. Just name it.

[Marilyn is silent.]

DOOKIE: Anything you want.

[MARILYN: *(Pause.)* You speak French?]

DOOKIE: What?

[MARILYN: French. You know anything about it. The words. Accents. Anything?]

DOOKIE: No. Why you ask?

[MARILYN: I just thought, if I was gonna marry somebody, they were gonna speak French, that's all.]

DOOKIE: That ain't a problem.

[MARILYN: You just admitted you can't speak a lick.]

The Legacy

Mark Harelik

Scene: a small town on the plains of West Texas, 1962

Serio-Comic
Nathan: (12) a young boy preparing to make his Bar Mitzvah

> *Nathan must learn how to make his Bar Mitzvah by listening
> to an old LP recording made by his grandfather many years
> before. Frustrated by the poor quality of the recording,
> Nathan here draws an impertinent analogy to his predica-
> ment.*

NATHAN: So here's the deal. Moses went way to the top of this
mountain, 'cause he was gonna meet God up there. And it was
this really big deal, 'cause God was gonna tell him what all the
Jews were supposed to believe from there on out. It was like this
big agreement where God tells Moses, Moses tells everybody
else, and if they all stuck to the rules, God would be their big pro-
tector and everything. It was called a co-ve-nant. Okay. So here's
Moses, tramping to the top of the mountain, and he's got a big
problem. He's led this whole tribe of Israelites out into the middle
of this complete desert. And it wasn't a tribe like at the pic-
tureshow with a few Indians and some teepees, there was like
half a million people out there and they weren't very happy about
it, either.

So the pressure's on. He hikes up to the very top, takes him
all day, and when he arrives, there's nothing there. Rocks. Dirt.
That's it. Not even a view, 'cause he's surrounded by this dense
cloud that gets darker and darker right in the middle of the day.
Then lightning starts flashing all around, thunder crashes in his
ears. Now, here's where they say even though Moses couldn't see
God, he could hear Him. And that's how he took dictation and
got the ten commandments. But look, that guy was up there for

forty days, and all he came back with was ten little command-ments? Did God talk really slow? Did Moses keep screwing up the tablets with his chisel? No. Here's what I think happened. Out of the dark and the thunder and the wind, Moses heard a voice, and it sounded like this:

(He sets the needle on the record and we hear the old man chanting.)

NATHAN: "Excuse me, God, what?…I'm…I'm sorry…what?…Is that—what is that, Hebrew? I'm sorry, I only speak Egyptian. God? Oh, God!"

(The voice drones on, Nathan speaks over it.)

NATHAN: But God rattled on in His holy language about all sorts of important stuff, life-and-death stuff, and Moses just sat there like a grade A, number one goof, not understanding a single word. *(He lifts the needle from the record.)* Well, you know what he felt like? He felt like some miserable little twelve-year-old kid from west Texas who has to study for his bar mitzvah by mail order! A whole nation is waiting down below for him to bring back the miracles, and he's stuck in the wrong language. So what does he do? The only thing he *can* do. He memorizes that voice syllable by syllable and mumbledy by bumbledy and just hopes some-body'll figure it out later. *That's* what took so long. It was the world's first bar mitzvah lesson. I'm continuing a great tradition. *(A rumble of thunder, then a knocking is heard.)*

The Maiden's Prayer

Nicky Silver

Scene: a grand house in the country

Dramatic
Taylor: (20s) a man with a history of substance abuse and sexual experimentation

> *Taylor has cleaned-up his act and settled down with Cynthia, who is devoted to making their life together perfect. The happy couple has moved into Taylor's family home in the country where they are expecting the arrival of their first child. Here, the formerly dissolute Taylor confesses that he's finally found peace in the country.*

TAYLOR: *(Sitting on the ground.)* And I love it here.

[CYNTHIA: Really?]

TAYLOR: I never noticed it was beautiful. I never really looked around.

[CYNTHIA: It is.]

TAYLOR: God, I hated it growing up. My father loved it, which is probably why I didn't. He loved this house. Knocked down what was here before and built it himself—before I was born, of course, but I heard the stories. All those bedrooms were for brothers and sisters that never got born. That was when he thought she loved him, my mother that is. When she was well-behaved and he could still pretend.

[CYNTHIA: She didn't?]

TAYLOR: She didn't. But when I was little she was quiet and played along. I guess it was hard, or frustrating, because gradually, she started to speak. Just tiny stabs at first, but then huge vicious, disorganized attacks. My father retaliated by getting smaller and smaller until you couldn't find him. But he did love this house. We used to have picnics right here and Dad would say, "This is perfect. Bury me here. I want to be buried right here when I die." And mother replied, "Why wait?"

The Maiden's Prayer

Nicky Silver

Scene: a grand house in the country

Dramatic
Taylor: (20s) a man with a history of substance abuse and sexual experimentation

> *When Cynthia suffers a miscarriage, their marriage slowly deteriorates. Eventually, Cynthia leaves Taylor, who is tempted to revert to his previous lifestyle of substance abuse. Here, he tells his best friend that he no longer wishes to live.*

TAYLOR: That was before. I hope you're not going to lecture me. I hope you didn't come all this way to "talk" to me. I mean I appreciate the good intentions. But please don't. I know you care about me. I care about you. My God, we've known each other since we were six years old. But, I have to tell you I won't be "talked to." Do you understand?

[PAUL: Yes.]

TAYLOR: Because I'm doing what I want.

[PAUL: I just wish there was something…]

TAYLOR: *(Flat, not sad.)* You see the thing is, I know that I'm killing myself. I paid attention at those meetings. I took everything in. But I find, and please don't over-react, because it's just the way it is, I find that I don't really *want* to live any more.

[PAUL: Taylor.]

TAYLOR: I sound stupid probably. But there you are. I wouldn't worry too much. I don't have a lot of courage. I was never the type to really do things for myself. Went to work for my father. Dried out for Cynthia. So I wouldn't worry. The other day I took out a gun. My father had guns. Did you know that? A man who made toys for a living collected guns. I went up, into the attic and dug one out. A little gun, a pistol. And I held it and I looked at it.

It was sort amazing to me. I mean this small piece of metal that I held in my hand had so much power...But then I put it away... She might come back. People come back. I wish she would call.

Manson

Mark Roberts

Scene: the prison cell of Charles Manson

Dramatic
Charles Manson: (60s)

> *Here, infamous Charlie shares a psychedelic memory of his*
> *time in the wilderness in which he received his first "vision"*
> *of Helter Skelter.*

MANSON: It is a bad bad habit with a most curious effect. Life.
Doglife and apelife…the disappointed man speaks—I sought
great human beings, I found nothing but the apes of their Ideal.
In out in out, Listen…A question: Have you ever been awoken
from a sweet dream by the heavy sigh of a fellow sleeper? Have
you ever been flung from the gate of Heaven and awoken in a
sea of twisted limbs where the air is high with the scent of sweat
and the sound of others' breathing and another day is drawing
close, another day of questions and opinions and voices talking
to me and voices talking at me.

We—the kids and I—were staying at the Barker ranch, a run-
down place on the desert's edge and another day such as this, so
like many others, drew close, a day on which everything that had
been came to an end. I rose from the darkness in which we lay,
sustaining each other in each other's tainted air, and while the
children slept the sleep of the stoned, I picked my way through
the sway of stiff dicks and slack jaws and decided to follow in the
steps of…Our Lord Messiah. The Word, The Word made Flesh,
Flesh with a taste for the hot desert sun, and, oh yes, the fear of
death itself. The fear of Jesus, the fear of death, the fear of a
worm gnawing in your head *(Singsong.)* when you're dead when
you're dead!

I speak no lies. I decided—as I entered the dawn—to go

where He had once been alone. The desert. Alone. Alone in the desert. Into the desert, this way, it's, all you have to do, put one foot in front of the other. I watched as the sun edged over the Panamint Mountains, the sky dissolving through blue, azure, sapphire, to turquoise where a divine and bloody hand drew its bleeding fingers across the span of Heaven, I watched the sun and every desert that had ever been heated by it or chilled by the moon lay before me that morning. And I walked and I walked in the cool of the morning 'till I reached the basin of Death Valley—where *I* would not fear the shadow of death—to see a whole new range of mountains up ahead.

The desert plays tricks with the eyes and what seemed like a flat twelve mile stretch was indeed forty or more. But I knew the desert and I knew its tricks. A boulder, a bush—in the day, walk by its sunny side for in its shade the rattlesnakes lay cooling their tails—at night walk by the other side for that's where the sun'd been, and that's where the serpents warmed the'selves by night on the baking sand. One of the many things man and the serpent have in common. When it's hot they want it cold, when it's cold they want it hot. Listen. Listen to my footfall in the sand.

I tied a bandanna about my head and a jacket round my waist—and I grinned and I laughed as the minutes turned to hours and I left the whole world behind me. Ha! to breathe such air as this. No kids, no cops, no coons, nothing to smoke or swallow only crisp clean air. The kind you can't get when all the other addicts are about. The further I went, the sweeter the air, the sweeter the air the faster I went, and further and further until…mid-morning and the fucking, freakin' sun decided to spin about in the sky casting its heat as it turned on itself in insy-binsy circles.

I sat down, sweat slip-sliding down my spine and said to myself, 'There is no way back, without first going forward.' I resolved to walk to the mid-point, halfway between Death Valley basin and the mountains. I stood up—walk, walk this way—my legs beginning to ache some yet I was nowhere near the mid-point and, meanwhile, the sun was cooking in the sky, turning up the heat, moment by moment as it turned towards its three o'clock high. Jesus Christ, you and me both man, escaping from the real-world and into the shimmering haze of self-inflicted thirst and heat and pain. Twelve o'clock was drawing near, but the mountains were not, walk as I did, the mountains seemed as far away as ever. 'Could I live here?' I asked myself. 'You could!' Another voice, not an echo, another voice spoke to me. I stopped, I could see it from the corner of my eye, a shadow on the sand, I turned, quick—and it was still out of the corner of my eye. 'Who the fuck are you?' 'Who am I? I am behind you when you walk ahead, ahead when you walk backwards.' I fell silent, slowly raised my arm, the shadow stretched his and said, 'I have put words in your mouth and covered you with the shadow of my hand—I who set the Heavens in place, who laid the foundations of the Earth—' And my shadow vanished from the sand, and where it had been, in the ground, was an entrance to a hole.

I knelt down at the hole and asked, 'Could I live here?' Another voice, not an echo, another voice, 'You could!' From that moment on, nothing could have been clearer. The time was drawing near. Helter Skelter. Formula of my happiness: a yes, a no, a straight line, a goal…It was beginning, the beginning of the end of the world as it was before the coming of Me. Satan could've stood there and showed me the riches of the world, I'd have laughed, said, 'Fuck you, Satan, I am the King of the World, do not offer me what is already rightfully mine.'

I left a pile of stones—a marker to show me where the hole was, a hidey hole to which I would return to arise when the time is right, for if I was going to set the world ablaze, I was gonna learn from the serpent: seek the shade…But I still had not reached the mid-point. Each step was a journey into pain and soon I was flat-footin' it like a wino across the jittery sand, until—ahead—a small hedge—I went to it and spread my jacket across its spikey arms—enough shadow to lay down and cover my face. Oh joy of joys! licked my lips—rough tongue over two cracked cups. I saw a pebble, the size of a pea and remembered the old Red Indian trick. I rolled the pebble about the inside of my mouth and I started to salivate. Onwards, onwards, my tongue working the pebble about my mouth and then, a dry pebble, a dry tongue, a dry mouth.

The next time I stopped, it was three o'clock. I was in the middle, I looked ahead, I looked back—the mid-point of the desert and time to turn back. Returning to the world, I was not the same man, oh no! After a while I fell into the habit of falling over every five minutes or so, at first picking myself up but then I fell over and I tried to crawl bu'th'sand and the rocks were too hot and hard to hold, so I picked myself up—by now, the air was not so sweet—and I fell. Face down in the dust, six o'clock, the sun as hot as ever and it occurred to me—'Charlie, you're a dead man!' I didn't have the energy to arise. I lay there, hands beneath my head to keep my tongue out of the dust.

The dying man finally raised his face to speak his final words. I opened my eyes and there I saw a rock. I gave it the benefit of my thoughts. 'You lucky bastard, you don't have life, so you don't know what it's like to suffer, be hungry or thirsty or worry about living or dying. You're dead, you som-of-a-bitch, dead!' I turned over on my back and the sun—the sun that had been spinning above me in the sky—the sun dipped over the mountains.

And I gave up. No more Charlie, no Helter Skelter. I followed in the footsteps of Christ and wound up deep in my own asshole. I looked at the rock and registered a plea, a prayer from the dying. 'Help me, I don't want to die yet.' How that rock was beloved by God. 'You lucky fucker...' I was mad, desperate, 'You don't *know* pain!' And then, the strangest thing occurred. I laughed. Out loud. I caught myself chuckling in the back of my scorched throat, I laughed, I laughed aloud, a tear rolled down my cheek and moistened the edge of my lips. I lay there and laughed. There I was, arguing with a goddamned rock. I laughed and realized a simple truth—dying men do not laugh like this. I had made a simple error. It wasn't me on the point of death. It was you. Laughter brought me to my feet, made me strong, pushed me forward, and as I walked I was certain of The Truth. The Time was Now. Helter Skelter—comin' down fast...

When the night came down I lay between the warmth of two boulders and listened to the silence. There was no moon and no stars. I had only one dream I recall. The world was on fire and I walked through the flames untouched, unscathed; I awoke the next morning with a smile. When I finally returned to the ranch, the kids came flying at me from all directions. Every mouth was moving at me, and their eyes wandered each inch of my battered flesh in disbelief. 'Here he is!' 'Where ya been?' 'Shappenin'?' Lazarus never knew such a greeting. Voices voices voices…and then…silence…and then, a single voice…'Where ya been, Charlie?' 'Don't ask me where I've been, man, ask me where I'm going.' 'Where ya going, Charlie?' 'Los Angeles.'

Marcus is Walking

Joan Ackerman

Scene: the simplest car possible

Serio-Comic
Henry: (30s) a man in love

> *After making love with Lisa for the first time (In the back seat of his car, no less.), Henry makes the following declaration of love.*

HENRY: Lisa, I love you.

[LISA: Henry…]

HENRY: I do.

[LISA: You don't have to say that.]

HENRY: But I do. Love you. For me not to say it, not to acknowledge it, would be like not acknowledging a little rain cloud inside the car, pouring rain. There *isn't* one, but if there *were* one, it would be very odd not to comment on it. Actually, it feels kind of like a storm, in my system, my world, these emotions, that I have for you. They're terribly distracting, I can't focus properly, can't do *anything* really without this constant disturbance, like a swarm of bees inside and outside me…this tumultuous…uh…*obsession* with you. It's hard to describe. Sometimes, when I'm with you, Lisa, I feel like there are three people in the room: you, me and this…tangle of emotions zooming around in insane patterns like protons, neutrons, racing, this sculpture that I happen to be carrying around inside me. You know I'm normally pretty witty, my friends think I'm funny, but when I'm with you my…I just…my tongue just gets shipwrecked on my teeth. I have to say that it's not entirely *pleasant* being so completely uncontrollably smitten by you. There's actually quite a bit of pain involved that…a *lot* of pain I can't do much about, but…Lisa…you touch something so deep in me…I felt it the instant I met you, I had to run out of the room...your voice, your language, these phrases you come up with—"loaded for bear," "boarding-house reach" when you reached across me in the conference room for pizza, "boarding-house reach" I love that, it just *sends* me, how you talk, your eyes, your handwriting. Physically, I find you incredibly sexy but that is the least of it...your sense of...I'm babbling but...if I can just at least try to express...I just need to tell you no one has ever made me feel the way that you do...I know I realize it's my problem, I'm not dumping all this on you, I'm the one who has to deal with it but, I...I *am* in love with you.

Martini

Richard Lay

Scene: a bar in NYC

Dramatic
Paul: (20s) a young man who has everything, except a future

> *This wealthy young executive has been diagnosed with a brain tumor. Here he sips a martini and wonders aloud if he should still propose to his girlfriend.*

PAUL: *(Holding a martini and cigar in hand. Arrogant.)* I have a JOB on Wall Street. I drink MARTINIS and I smoke CIGARS…I have a girlfriend from the Upper East Side. Her name is Laura and we shop together on Saturdays at Barney's up-town…oh yes, and so that I don't forget, I drive a black MERCEDES and I work out every day at a TOP gym in Chelsea. These *(Flex.)* biceps are very, very expensive… *(Deep sigh.)* But I do have a problem. Yesterday, or it might have been the day before, I was diagnosed with a brain tumor…And it's a REAL one, not the benign Elizabeth Taylor type. *(Smirks.)* But as I am INVINCIBLE I'm trying to shove it out of my mind. *(Proudly.)* It IS advanced—but I can afford a TOP surgeon… *(Clears throat.)* My other problem is that I planned to propose to Laura on bended knee this weekend at her parents townhouse where we will sleep together on satin sheets while her Mummy and Daddy go to the opera…And you might like to know that Gentleman's Quarterly featured me last month as the young man most likely to be the first billionaire under thirty in the year 2000. *(Pause and cough.)* Laura's brother wrote the article and I appeared on chat shows and signed some autographs for IMPOR-TANT people…Life is so good and nothing must change just because of a silly blob of out-of-control cells doing their thing inside my head…So I plan to go ahead to proposing and giving her a twenty-thousand dollar diamond ring from Tiffany's—but do I tell her about my little problem? Reason says I should but if I do will she vanish… *(Soft laugh.)* Laura's not EXACTLY a Florence Nightingale type…just a Jewish Princess who owns lots of gold and extremely expensive clothes… *(Four-second pause.)* …I don't consider the possibility of dying—well, it's not REALLY a possibility for someone like me, is it? Me with the Midas touch and the good looks born to rule, whatever circumstances I'm in…my headaches and dizziness I had put down to sinus. But then I started walking sideways without meaning to and one eye lid sort of drooped and sometimes I had trouble differentiating between my dreams and reality—just off and on…not every day. I blamed Martinis…But one day I was holding onto walls to stand up and I couldn't remember my name. That was last year…last month… last Tuesday…not long ago…I don't KNOW when. *(Controlled desperation.)* …do I still ask her to marry me…I know, I know, I know—I've got it…Laura, who's going to be my wife. Yes, Laura, bended knee, opera…I have to sit down and have a martini and a cigar—what order, maybe a cigar and a martini—there's that, isn't there—that to consider. *(Sits.)*

Molly's Delicious

Craig Wright

Scene: an apple orchard in Pine City, Minnesota. Autumn, 1965

Serio-Comic
Jerry: (18) a young soldier on leave from the war in Vietnam

> *Jerry has returned to Pine City from Vietnam to discover that
> Alison, his girlfriend, is carrying his child. When he prepares
> to do the right thing and proposes, Alison balks, soliciting the
> following confession.*

JERRY: Can I tell you something?

[ALISON: What?]

JERRY: I was thinking in town, you know: I'm brave about everything but you.

[ALISON: Yeah?]

JERRY: Yeah. I had a whole ship run over me once when I was
working in a buoy cage in the Marshall Islands, and I wasn't half
as scared then, bouncing and clanking around underneath that
ship as I am whenever I get around you. And darlin', believe me,
I know exactly what you mean about me being gone all the time,
I know it's not a good way to be married. My Dad was a Coastie
and he was never around, and when my Mom died, I had to keep
her casket in the house for two weeks waiting for him to get
clearance to come home and see her. So I know it's not ideal. I
do. But darlin', I gotta be honest with you. When I die, and my
mind flips back through the pages, trying to find what really mattered? If I had to pick which moments to look at right before I
slipped away, I know every one of those moments would be on a
ship in the middle of the ocean, because that's the only place my
soul is really satisfied. I mean, I can talk a good game back here
in polite society, and I do like a pretty girl—well, one pretty girl in
particular—but at heart?—I'm a sailor. And like my Daddy used

to say to me, "Sailors belong on ships and ships belong at sea."
And it's true. I love you SO much darlin'…but I don't know what
I'd become if I left the service—probably some sort of monster.
And that wouldn't be good for you or Junior.

[ALISON: But it won't be good for us if you get killed, either.]

JERRY: Darlin', I won't get killed. I promise. Look, you want this
war to end? Let me go. Send me back. Let me do my job and I
guarantee you in six months time there won't be one American
soldier left over there. Westmoreland and all those fellas in the
big pants club, they got it all worked out. And I'll come home in
three years to you and Junior and we'll be stationed in Groton or
San Francisco or who knows where—

[ALISON: *(Cutting in a little enthusiastically.)* I'd like to go to
San Francisco.]

JERRY: Then that's where we'll go! That's exactly where we'll go!
Just tell me when I come home that you and Junior'll be waiting.
It's just three years away, Darlin'. Every kind of happiness you ever
dreamed of us having is just three years away. Can't you hold on
til then? Please? I love you so much. Please?

Mud, River, Stone

Lynn Nottage

Scene: the lobby of the Hotel Imperial, somewhere in Africa

Dramatic
Joaquim: (20s) a former soldier now the bellboy of a crumbling
old hotel

> *Made desperate by personal privation and the constant polit-*
> *ical upheaval in his country, Joaquim has taken a handful of*
> *guests hostage at the dilapidated Hotel Imperial. In a quiet*
> *moment, this frustrated young African reveals the pathology*
> *of his growing sense of emotional nihilism.*

JOAQUIM: All I want is to be a civil servant, have a suit and ride the
bus to my office building. Seven stories, the tallest office building
in the city. Have a telephone and an ink pen. A commode. I could
have read good, but the war came to my village. And took me
away. Ten years, you know. My father was a farmer. His father. His
father. It was my destiny. But the war was all around us, in the
stories of men who spoke of it with respect. The war was a distant monster, too far away to make me scared. Then men without limbs began to appear and beggar children wept for food.
The sound of gun fire rippled through the forest. Rat, tat, tat, tat.
And the war was upon us. I was the youngest son, I was given up
to the rebels to fight for freedom. It was either bullets or children.
And children are less valuable. Ten years later, we are victorious,
and I am not a child. My village is a clearing in the forest, taken
by the war. And the land is barren, there are no farmers left. This
peace is a curse. There is too much time to think. *(A moment.)* I
was a good soldier. Do you know what it means to have been a
good soldier? I was told that things would be better if we won.
That the man with the glorious voice spoke the truth.

Narcissus & Echo

Book and Lyrics by Jeff Goode
Music by Larrance Fingerhut

Scene: ancient Greece, or thereabouts

Serio-Comic
Cupid: (any age) God of love

> *Here, this cherubic cutie reveals some interesting facts regarding his modus operandi.*

CUPID: HELLO! My name is Cupid. Demigod of love. Do you mind if I smoke? Which reminds me of an old joke: "Do you smoke after sex?" "Only for a few minutes, till I cool down." B'dum Bum. So people ask me what I do for a living. I say "cause trouble." Heh heh. Although, where I really make the big bucks is modeling for Valentine candy wrappers. Maybe you've seen this one. *(Poses as baby cupid.)* I know, it's not quite the same without the diaper and the bow and arrows. I used to pose nude, but I don't want to turn up on a webpage. Which by the way, I wanted to clear up this thing about the bows and arrows. 'Cause I don't know whose idea that was, but it was not me. Because, first of all, my aim is lousy. With a shotgun, maybe, but if I had to use a bow and arrow…Let's just say, There would be a lot more people with free time on the weekends. And have you ever been shot with an arrow? Trust me: Not very Romantic. No. We use chemicals. I know what you're thinking. "This guy doesn't look like a chemist." Hey, fuck you! *(Catching himself.)* I'm sorry. I'm sorry. As Demigod of Love I gotta be careful saying that to large groups of people. Actually, no, the boys down at the lab do most of the work. I mainly handle distribution. Usually we use large public water supplies. If anybody notices, we tell 'em it's Fluoride. It's hard to figure exact dosages on a lake, though, so we have been known to make mistakes. Which is why I don't recommend you drink the water in Chicago. And keep a safe distance from anyone who does. Anyway, I just wanted to come down and clear up a few things: The stuff is NOT addictive. *(Beat.)* Okay. It's addictive. I don't use the stuff myself. Bad for business. You ever seen the movie Scarface? Besides which, I'm allergic. Gives me a rash and then I throw up. I know some of you have that reaction, too. Sorry. We're working on it. So anyway, I just wanted to clear up these things about the bow and arrow and all before we get started. Thanks a lot. You've been great. I love you guys. Just kiddin', I told you I never touch the stuff.

Narcissus & Echo

Book and Lyrics by Jeff Goode
Music by Larrance Fingerhut

Scene: ancient Greece, or thereabouts

Serio-Comic
Narcissus: (20s) a young nymph.

> *Here, Narcissus encounters his own reflection and is appropriately impressed.*

NARCISSUS: Gosh now I'm hot…and thirsty, too. I hope no one sees me drink out of this pond. *(Narcissus starts to take a drink from the pond.)* Yah! Oh, it's a water sprite. You scared the heck outta me! Well, hel-*lo!* You're kinda cute.

> [CUPID: "…and as he cast himself down, exhausted, on the grassy verge to slake his thirst, he fell in love with his reflection."]

NARCISSUS: Say, handsome, where have you been all my life? What? I'm sorry, I was talking while you were talking, what? Listen, you wanna go somewhere and get a drink? What am I thinking? You're standing in a pool of water and I offer you a drink! You must think I'm such an airhead. *(Giggles.)* Mmm-hnh, you are a sweet thing, though. Honey, why don't you come on up here and give me a big wet one. Playing hard to get, huh? *(Grabs it.)* Hey, where'd you go? Oh, jeez. I finally find someone who interests me, and I scare him away. Oh, there you are. Oh, you wanna dance. *(Dances with the shimmering reflection, gradually slowing down.)* That was nice. I…I know this may seem premature, but…I really think I love you. I never thought I could love a man…I never thought I could love anyone again…but you…I don't know, I feel like I know you. *(Nodding.)* You know what I mean? Do you get that feeling? Me, too. Do you want to kiss me? *(Tries to kiss it.)* Yow, this water is cold! Where'd you go?

What, more dancing? *(Dances.)* You're good. *(After the dance.)* You never get tired, do you? So, tell me about yourself. *(Pause.)* Or not. That's okay. Well, okay, I'll start...My name is Narcissus. My parents were the River-God Cephisus...

A Night at the Blowhole

Robert Coles

Scene: a backroom booth store known as "The Blowhole"

Serio-Comic
Louis: (40s) an edgily neurotic man in search of his lover

> *Louis has recently begun to suspect that Edwin's nightly jog
> is more than it seems. This night he has followed Edwin on
> his nightly run with disastrous results. Here, he describes his
> traumatic experience to a friend whom he has called for help.*

LOUIS: Harvey: Read my lips! I *saw* Edwin come in here! *(He
releases Harvey.)* Somehow, tonight-…I don't know why, maybe
some wise little voice inside called out "Don't trust him anymore"—but tonight I decide to follow Edwin on his jog.

[HARVEY: He didn't see you?]

LOUIS: See *me?* I could barely see *him*. He can run really fast. I was
huffing and puffing like crazy just to stay within two blocks of
him.

[HARVEY: So he *was* running.]

LOUIS: At *first*. Just long enough to get out of the neighborhood.
I thought I'd lost him. Especially after I tripped over that
Pomeranian.

[HARVEY: You tripped over a—]

LOUIS: I was ready to give up and go home. My breathing was very
shallow, my heart rate had increased alarmingly and there was a
shooting pain in my underarm region—it could have been a col-
lapsed lung, but something told me to press on. So I plodded forward, even as I examined the ugly bruise on my hip where I'd
fallen on that hideous little dog. *Then,* just as I looked up from
my wound, *there* he was. He'd stopped jogging and he was simply…loitering. Throwing furtive glances over each shoulder as if
to see if "the coast was clear." I immediately ducked into a door-

way of a store, not more than fifteen feet away. Then all it once it became clear. As I turned to my left and gazed through the shop's plate glass window, I saw the gleaming nickel studs of harness reflecting the flashing colors of the passing cars. Then, beneath it, emerging from the open front of a really exquisitely-crafted pair of leather chaps, was the biggest, most frighteningly realistic dildo I've ever seen. I was standing in front of The Blowhole!!!!

> [HARVEY: Oh! You were in front of the little gift shop they run next door!]

LOUIS: And *Edwin* was standing in front of the door to the *backroom boothstore!* The door you and I just came through!

> [HARVEY: Actually, I suppose you wouldn't call it a "gift shop." I mean, I guess I wouldn't do my Christmas shopping there. Heh heh heh. *(Harvey chuckles at his little joke, then seriously reconsiders.)* Hmmm. Well, maybe that depends on who I was buying gifts *for...*]

LOUIS: *Harvey!* Shut up! I'm not finished! When I saw the dildo, I realized: *this* is where Edwin *goes* every night! And as I cautiously poked my head out to look again, I *saw* him come in here!

> [HARVEY: Omigosh, you must have been stunned.]

LOUIS: I was paralyzed with confusion. What to do? What to do? There was only one answer.

> [HARVEY: Come and get *me.*]

LOUIS: Well, I *realized,* Harvey, that I was only two blocks from your place. You have to understand my mental state. Seventeen years of marriage, and it was all a farce! Can you blame me for reaching out for help, for what I at least *assumed* would be the *support* of my best friend?

> [HARVEY: And you *have* it, Louis, you *have* it. I'm *here,* aren't I? I wouldn't come into a place like this for just *anyone.* I know you're *suffering,* and I'll help in any way I can.

LOUIS: *(Responds with very dramatic sincerity.)* Thank you, Harvey. Thank you for that. I won't forget it. I won't forget that you were there in my time of grief.

Noah's Archives

Stephen Spoonamore

Scene: a bar

Serio-Comic
Shem: (30–40) a man contemplating his life's love

> *Here, earthy Shem reveals uncanny insight into the nature of love.*

SHEM: I don't really have much to say about love. I know I don't understand it. I know that. I can tell you it is not: Honeysuckles and Watercress and Posies. It's not sighs and backlighting and extensively scored with violins and full woodwinds. Parts maybe. Maybe. Look at the sentiments of lovers recorded from another time tell us…how fucked the whole sentiment thing is. Lovers thoughts from another time rarely seem anything but tarnished cutlery of sickening and dated patterns set aside and unused since some brides death. At best. But still, when I am there and I feel all the more present because I am with her. I think myself in the presence of the the other half of something…A wise man I talked with once told me: "the Dominant emotion of any good marriage is tolerant and distant indifference." As a younger man I jolted at such a self said declaration but in the next moment knew it was true. "Punctuated I hope by moments of Joy?…Happiness?…Love?" I asked. "No. Not Love. Happiness and Joy of course, in the best cases of course, but not love. No. No, Love is not something to find together but to have apart. Perhaps when your beloved is sleeping you may love them but never allow the love to shred. Ration it. Hide it. Make it a puzzle to be unwound over a lifetime." "Like buried treasure." I said. "No." He said, "Like a sewer pipe. Your life is wonderful while it's buried, stinking hell when it's not." Love really isn't much. But do we go on about it. A warmth in the chest and the head and the loins…Love is better understood in it's absence and is perhaps only given scale by the loss of the loved. I have a beloved. She isn't with me. I don't know if I have a love greater or lesser than any other but I know I am a better person when I am with her. And I know I do not feel whole with her away. And she is…away. I…don't really have any good words. "I am a better person when I am with you." I told her that. Yea. Sober. Being a chick she, of course, thinks I don't tell her I love her often enough. So it's like she's always pointing to the sewer pipe saying "dig it up dig it up dig it up!" And you're saying no! It's a sewer pipe I was warned not to! And she's "Dig it up! dig it up! dig it up!" And your "ahhhh!" Life is fine why make a stinking hell! I think it's partly genetic in men. And I just can't hear the word. Love. Love. I love you. I don't sound like him but when I say it, I just hear my dad saying "I love you honey" every time he left home, and then see me mother laying in bed and crying for a month without eating when he left her without even a note. I don't know. Could sour you on the whole thing, but I just got twitchier about the word. Like saying it will make it end. But every woman wants to hear it every day. And so she thinks I don't say it enough. Maybe I don't. But she is the only one I think makes me a better person, we see two different facets of the same world, facets that add up from each other. So I say I love you, for you. I write at the end of notes, I love you, for you. You mean enough to me that I say it and write and even think it, an in doing I walk into a realm where I don't know what I mean when I do. But to be my partner. She asked me to say it more. And I want her. Sometimes though. I wake up so much earlier than she does. I see her asleep. And I know I love her. She is all there and mine and I love her. And I know how much it will hurt me when she is gone. And she is gone. Well, I haven't woken up next to her in five months. When one is gone. When she is gone. And she is gone. The remaining Lover finally understands what love was. And rather than watching you sleep, or sleeping so you can watch me, I'm out here waiting on my hooligan friends. Chasing pussy. Sure everyone is. It's why we're out. I flirt and play along too. I don't want to catch any, but it is why we're out. And I have a hole inside me that every time I flirt seems even larger, and I flirt and think the whole time. I wish I was with you. I wish you were not far away. I wish I understood why you need to be. I wish you were asleep beside me. I...I wish...the world was different.

Noah's Archives

Stephen Spoonamore

Scene: a bar

Serio-Comic
Shem: (30–40) a man contemplating his life's love

> *Shem here ruminates on the ultimately finite nature of human sexual relations.*

SHEM: After 25 years of sexual activity…what do I call this where I am at? A cross-roads? I don't know. I mean you find out that there are what? About five or six positions…and then…what? That's what there is and I guess I am wondering if that is the whole point…I mean sure there's this, and this one…and that… and then you get that side one with the legs sort of like that…I love how deep you get in that one…and you can see her face in profile, get a hand up on a breast…still enjoy her ass… that… well…and whatever. I mean sure Kama Sutra yah yah yah, some-thing weird on her birthday…yah yah yah…But it's still just varia-tions on the basic five or six and then you have different environments, You got the inside stuff, with beds and floors and Tubs and door jambs…then you go the outside stuff: woods and camping and seashore…You got the grit thing to deal with. Friction is the enemy of moving parts after all. But…I mean…I even did it on a ski slope sliding down in the middle of the night…just another variation of the me on my back her riding on top, just with the added toboggan thing. I don't recommend that variation. She got pregnant too. So maybe for some of you doing desperate breeder dancing…As I was saying. After twenty-five years of sexual activity, I find myself at this sort of…point…the point of liking the whole thing in idea but really dreading the actual thing…really…finding and then dancing and then "you brush this, I brush that. Lets arrange it so our legs touch for a while, I kiss you here, you kiss me there, you get wet, I get hard, I finger you, you get real wet, you grip me I get harder, One of the Six. Then shorten up on all that lead in, try the other Five. Switch off One four three. Six one Six on floor, Six one Six in bed, Six one Six in the tub...Why? And Why? Why all this? I don't know...Yada yada ya. I mean. I don't want kids...I am driving my mother fucking crazy that I don't, but any sane person doesn't. Today...I'm not the brightest bulb in the socket but I can read... Six billion of us. Six billion little resource destroyers...most of whom can't even read...So. I mean it's sex is for begetting...it's all just a big charade so egg and sperm can mix it up...Sex...I really do love the idea now. More than the sex. And I love happy couples. Which is new. Seeing happy couples. I wish I was them. Half of one. I saw this old couple, probably sixty or so white shirts, Khaki slacks, sunhats the whole LL Bean parental unit she looked at him and smiled and he made that chuckling guys make who look like that and have money and power and ease and that chuckle that says "I understand and everything is right with us right now" It was on the beach too. Sand, enemy of friction wasn't bothering them. That chuckle. I want that, and someone to give it to more than anything one through six. Though I'd like that too. One thru six, Chuckle. Chuckle, Six thru one. Sorry. I'm getting old.

On Golden Wings

A. Giovanni Affinitio

Scene: Milano, Italy. A winter evening in 1841

Dramatic
Giuseppe Verdi: (27) a young composer

> *Following the deaths of his beloved wife and children, Verdi has retreated into a world of grief and despair. When he is pressured by the Inspector General of the Royal and Imperial Austro-Hungarian Theatre to write a new opera, he is forced to reveal the depth of his sorrow.*

VERDI: It must be wonderful to be able to walk out of a room like this. Walk away from ugliness.

[MERELLI: There's always pain…everywhere, You didn't invent it. I'm sorry that was a mean remark.]

VERDI: *(Almost to himself.)* I was not permitted such freedom. I sat with her in a room where pain lived, day and night. She had hardly brushed the funeral dirt from her black dress before it was time to be soiled by it again. She was…tall. You noticed that right away about her. Funny, the trivial things that stick in your head.

(Verdi slumps on the piano stool. Merelli remains by the door facing upstage.)

VERDI: She seemed to grow visibly smaller as she followed each of the tiny coffins out of that room. First it was the boy. The doctors never knew what it was. They just showed us their palms and stared up at the ceiling. I could do nothing, *nothing* but watch him waste away in his mother's arms as they clung together like two frightened children. A few days later it was the little girl's turn…my daughter of little years and big smiles. That same nameless sickness that ends in death. It was too much, too much. But still not enough. In the next month, my wife, she…was taken ill. A third coffin went out of that room, only this time I had to follow it alone. I was truly alone. Suddenly, everyone I loved in the world was gone…forever. Do you know how long forever is?

91

Patchwork "Lucky"

Vicki Mooney

Scene: a junk shop

Serio-Comic
Lucky: (30–40) an ex-junkie

> *Lucky has created an emotionally comfortable niche for him-*
> *self in the junk trade. Discarded coffee makers, radios and*
> *the like enjoy special attention at Lucky's place, where hope-*
> *fully they can be rehabilitated and resold. Here the philo-*
> *sophical junkman describes meeting the love of his life at a*
> *methadone clinic.*

LUCKY: I find things. I fix 'em up. I provide a useful service. People throw out a vacuum cleaner. I fix it up with a twenty cent part and it's worth something. Toasters, same thing, only you see a toaster about every day. You never know what life will give you to work with. You never know what's gonna turn up tomorrow. Could be the chance of a lifetime, could be garbage. You never know. My old lady, she don't want me to be a junk dealer no more. Ellie says I gotta do something legal. Now that she's clean she's right on top of what's legal. That's where I found her, you know, in with the junk. Lucky for her I got an eye for potential. She's clean now, good as brand new. I met Ellie first at the methadone clinic. I go down to get my dose—on the program, doin' right, gettin' by. They tell me this is a lifetime deal. Tough goddamn counselors, and they're all on it, too. For the rest of your life, that's what they tell me! You're still an addict, you're just on something else—a legal substance—that's the only differ-ence, and you're never supposed to get off of it. Is that a load of shit or what? I mean, I go into the program cause I wanta get clean, not swap one bad habit for another. Anyway, I'm standing there waiting for my urine analysis to come back and this girl comes up to the window to cop her dose and I think; like, what's she doing here? You know? She looked so together, and I mean middle class—upper middle class together, like she knew how to take care of herself. I found her on Good Friday. Not this Good Friday, from a couple of years ago. I was scrounging around over by the Pier. I love the river. It's a good place to go—you go before the traffic gets started and it's kinda mystical. So I'm down there, I see this ratty looking furry somethin' in this pile of telephone poles. I'm thinkin': dead dog. Right? No. It was my girlfriend. My girlfriend to be if you wanta get technical. So, I go roll her over and it's Ellie from the clinic. I say: Ellie, you okay? She blows some chunks. I say: Want me to call you an ambulance? She says: *(Drunkenly.)* Take me home, I'll make you breakfast. She's drunk. Drunk, I can cope with. A hangover, I can handle. So, I bring her back to my place; put her in the shower. I stay right by her side until she wakes up again. Give her some juice, an aspirin. She goes back to sleep it off and I know she's not going to aspirate herself or nothin'.

I walk down the block. The Cleaners will not touch the fur jacket. Pretty disgusting, but I bet if I came in there wearing' a chauffeur's uniform, they would'a took it. No questions asked. Stop by the bodega. I make righteous chicken soup. Matzo balls that float. Mrs. Greenberg was my housemother at the Home. I peek in on Ellie and go work on my soup. Pretty soon my apartment smells like the Promised Land. Rich and steamy. Ellie comes around. I feel bad for her. She don't know where she is. She don't know who I am. Scared. Who can blame her? With a roaring, belching Night Train headache, added to it some vicious chops from peppermint schnapps. Hurtin'. You know how sorry you get after a night like that. How stupid you feel when you remember you coulda been rat bait. It's not like this was her first time, so she cries. I make her eat some chicken soup. She tells me I'm decent. So, what am I gonna do, lecture her? I been there. She says she ran into the old crowd. That always happens. They got no respect for what you're tryin' to do. You kick, they lose you. They will do anything to keep you on their level. I tell her she's too smart for that. I ask her where she's got to go. She cops to it. She's got no where. I tell her I'm not comin' on to her; she can use my couch. She don't remember me from the clinic, but hell, that morning she probably couldn't remember if she had an ass. I keep my word to her. She starts to flourish a little bit, which made me really happy. Kicked me up a step or two, which kicked her up a step or two, and here we are three years later. Makin' it. We take good care of each other. She's as good at it as I am. Personally, I think she could do better, but she says there ain't nobody better than me. Gotta be love, right?

The Pharmacist's Daughter

Monika Monika

Scene: Brooklyn, NY

Dramatic
Detective Reid: (30s) a dwarf who has just committed suicide

> *The death of his normal-sized brother, Dwayne, has driven
> Detective Reid to the ultimate act of grief and despair. After
> shooting himself in the heart, he uses his last breaths to
> explain his love of Dwayne.*

DETECTIVE REID: I was the only person on this earth that appreciated
Dwayne, he was terrible to me: insensitive, boring, fulla shit, but
the thing that made me love him was—he was that way to everybody. Before I was a detective I was the mascot for Crazy Eddie's
car deals on the local TV. I wore this cheap shit car salesman suit
and said we were short on staff but big on deals. I call my mother
and ask her what she thought of my television debut: she said I
had a good chin, I was wonderful. I asked this short girl: not a
dwarf,—I'd been chasing this skirt for years: What did you think?
She said I was very convincing, talented, obviously classically
trained—but wouldn't go out with me. I called my high school
drama teacher who always cast me as imaginary animals and
"Puck." He said I was terrific and got off the phone, quick. Then
I ask Dwayne: what do you think of the Crazy Eddie commercial
debut? He said, "You suck." Just like that. "You suck." Then he
drank all my beer, hung around my apartment and threw up all
over my bath towels. I love him for that. I quit the acting business,
got my PI license and it's all because of Dwayne. Now that he's
gone, I'll never have anybody say "you suck," again. It'll be
smoke and mirrors and "you have a good chin," "see you later,
midget." He used to call me "beanpole."

Polaroid Stories

Naomi Iizuka

Scene: a pier at the edge of the city, the late 1990s, night

Serio-Comic
D(Dionysus): (18–25) A partying God

> *The god of celebration has turned way hip in this adaptation*
> *of Ovid's Metamorphoses. Here D describes his first meeting*
> *with Oklahoma Boy, a spray and video junkie.*

D: this is how it begins, this is where—
i seen him out of nowhere, crazy amped out boy crazy oklahoma boy,
i found him up by port authority,
scheming and scamming, nickel diming what he can—
i watch him a while, see him get all's he can get,
and then he goes, he gets high on spray. oklahoma boy likes spray.
spray's cheap, he says, and then he smiles like a psychopath.
tell you what, he says to me, i ain't got a friend in this whole world,
are you my friend, he says to me,
what you got for me, friend? i got a kingdom, i says to him,
behold my kingdom, and he thinks that's the funniest thing.
he laughs so hard he falls down.
and then we get high. we fly.

oklahoma boy likes speed,
he likes it cause it makes him go so fast
it makes him go fucking speedracer fast with them fucking speed
racer eyes.
one night, he rips me off, digs around till he finds my stash,
i hear his fingers, i hear his eyes clicking in his head, i hear him
laughing in the dark
so high he can't hardly stand, he can't hardly breathe,
and then he takes my stuff, he goes away—

pockets full of quarters, he finds some arcade, video world is all
there is all there ever was, oklahoma boy disappears for days,
all speedracer eyes, big eyes, black as night, full of laser beams
and showers of light, galaxies and planets, whole worlds explod-
ing in his head, and it's so bright,
what it is, right, it's so bright, for a second you think you can see
then all there is is black—

Polaroid Stories

Naomi Iizuka

Scene: a pier at the edge of the city, the late 1990s, night

Serio-Comic
Narcissus: (20s) a self-infatuated young man

> *Here, a smooth-talking Narcissus gives a contemporary spin
> to the myth of Proteus.*

NARCISSUS: alright alright, here it is, alright, check it out: how i got
on the streets is like this: it's like this: once upon a time, like a
long time ago, i was left in this dumpster outside phoenix, i was
like a little baby, nobody wanted me, and then this pack of wild
dogs dug me out, fed me, took care of me, taught me how to
hunt and shit, i didn't know what human was—
ok ok never mind, that's b.s.
how it is, it's like this: i fell out of the sky over salt lake city, utah—
no wait, it's like this: i washed up on the shore of the mighty mis-
sissippi—
no wait, it's like this: i was left for dead in a room in palm springs
i was left for dead in a room in las vegas
i was left for dead in a parking lot in tucson
i was left for dead on the steps of the fucking lincoln memorial—
no wait up, wait up, that ain't how it goes—
ok, check it out, it's like this: i was left for dead in this stripmall
outside san ysidro, right, and this poor mexican family found me,
and took me back over the border to tj, and raised me as one of
their own
—nah, that ain't true neither, i'm just playin you.
what really happened, it's like this, and this is for real—
when i was like a little kid, the building where i lived at, it caught
on fire, mmhm, and my mother, she held me out the window,
and she was all like: "fly away fly away fly away, little bird," and

98

then she let go—only thing was, i wasn't no little bird, and i didn't fly, i fell, and i don't know what the bitch was smokin, cause if i didn't die from the fire, i shoulda straight up died from the fall— 'cept the thing being i landed on this big old mattress somebody threw out with the trash—fuckin fate, man, was on my ass—and then later this old wino found me, and took care of me for a while till his liver gave out, and then i was on my own, i was all alone, and that is the truth, i swear to god—

Private Eyes

Steven Dietz

Scene: here and now

Serio-Comic
Matthew: (30s) an actor whose wife is having an affair with their director

> *Here, Matthew finally gives voice to his suspicions as he confronts his wife and director with a monologue he later claims is new script material.*

MATTHEW: Okay, so I've been in the dark. I've been in the dark about this entire thing. And you've let me. You've let me stumble through darkness like an oaf in a cave. And perhaps you've said this to yourselves over time: "It's for his *own good.* Nothing good would come of him knowing more at this time. Let's do this for *him.* Let's keep a little *darkness* around him." And I thank you for that. For thinking of me with such regard. Because, it seems you've needed to get together quite often—sometimes even outside rehearsal, sometimes till very late at night—to make sure you were doing the *right thing* when it came to me. I'm in your debt for that. I truly hope that somehow, someday I can repay the both of you.

[Adrian and Lisa look quickly to each other, then say—]

[ADRIAN: Matthew—]

[LISA: Why don't—]

MATTHEW: Now, you are at a crossroads. You must take the next step. I'm aware of this and I don't envy your situation. At this moment, it must be said, that, for the first time in my life, I am completely thrilled to be *me.* Because my position is the simple one here. I lie in wait for you to enact your plan and then, holding cards you have no idea about, I play my hand. It's almost too easy. It's virtual baby candy. But, it's here and let's just accept it, shall we? Say: "Yes."

[LISA AND ADRIAN: Yes.]

MATTHEW: Good. One thing I ask of you. There is this *myth.* I'd like us to talk about it. The myth of which I speak is that of Telling the Truth Slowly Over Time. Now, this myth does have its proponents. They believe that the cold hard truth can, if rationed out slowly over time like, say, *cod liver oil,* be made more palatable. Perhaps even made attractive. Therapists do this. They are reluctant to come right out and say to a couple: "Tom, Jeanine, thanks for coming by today and here's my assessment of your relationship: It's fucked. Let it go. Say goodbye, divide up your stuff, and run for your lives." Why are they reluctant to do this? It would make them *obsolete.* Their jobs *depend* on giving out the truth at a *slower rate than it is actually needed.* They claim, of course (and are never challenged, since it is our fate to bow to anyone holding a weapon or a Ph.D.), that they are doing this for the couple's "own good"—that they are giving them the truth at a pace they can *"handle."* But, push has come to SHOUT and here we are: *(He moves closer to them.)* I urge you to take whatever truth is at your disposal and *divest* it. Cut it loose. All of it. Tell it fast and tell it now. It is not more *palatable,* it is not a *gift* to tell someone you love the Slow Truth, unless you happen to know they have a fondness for Slow Disease like, say, *cancer.*

[LISA: Matthew—]

MATTHEW: Our collisions with others are not measured events. They are *radical.* Our love and lust and all our aching wonder is radical. Affairs don't accrue methodically, they spring up like lightning—like lost tourists with cash in hand. They are *feverish.* They are *fast.* And if we try to come clean by Telling the Truth about them Slowly Over Time, we give birth to a *mutant truth.* A truth that bears no relation to the fierce hearts that we possess. *The truth we tell, and the way we tell it, must be as radical as our actions. (Pause.)* And so…Carol, Derek, what have you got to say for yourselves?

Private Eyes

Steven Dietz

Scene: here and now

Dramatic
Matthew: (30s) an actor whose wife is having an affair with their director

Matthew here reveals a dark fantasy about his wife's infidelity.

MATTHEW: This is what you must know about my wife:
My wife loves her wedding ring.
Sometimes I wake in the morning and catch her lying in bed next to me, holding her hand in the air, admiring her ring in the sunlight.
My wife never removes her wedding ring, with one exception: to wash the dishes. She places it carefully on a ledge above the sink. Then, when the dishes are done, she weds the ring to her finger once again.
I imagine she may also take it off to have her affair.
Therefore, this is my picture of her infidelity:
My wife is at the sink, holding a big yellow sponge.
She is doing the dishes.
There is a man *directly behind her.*
He is *not* doing the dishes.
Water gushes into the sink.
Steam glazes the windows.
My wife's hair has fallen across her face.
Her hands are red and wet.
Her fingers furrowed from this prolonged immersion.
With this man directly behind her, my wife washes every…last…dish…in…our…home.
Later, when I walk through the door, she looks up from her chair and smiles. "How was your day?" she asks, rubbing the lotion into her hands.

[Silence. Cory stares at him. He places the second side of dressing back in its place on the tray.]

MATTHEW: Have you nothing to say?

Reading the Mind of God

Pat Gabridge

Scene: Benatek Castle, near Prague, 1600

Dramatic
Johannes Kepler: (29) a brilliant astronomer

> *Kepler has recently arrived at Benatek Castle at the invitation of the great Tycho Brahe. Here he will join Brahe's team of astronomers who are in the process of charting the heavens as no one has done before. Kepler's first project is to chart Mars using data and instruments the likes of which he has never had access to before. Here, the passionate young man frantically makes new calculations on the Red Planet.*

KEPLER: Floating in empty space,
twisting in every direction,
hungry for my first true glimpse of Heaven,
courtesy of Tycho's generosity.
We join hands and pull each other
Towards greatness.
God has written his signature across the sky,
a map leading us to comprehend
the magnificence of his creation.

The planets move in circles around the sun.
Elegant simplicity.
Imagine God fixing earth in the center.
God does not create ugliness in the sky.

Five perfect solids.
A glimmer of an answer.
Six planets for the five solids.
Mercury and Venus fit so wonderfully.

Tiny steps towards comprehension,
numbers falling into place.
I will construct a platform
with Tycho's numbers,
supporting a hundred theories and ideas.
If only Mars would cooperate.

Eccentric circles.
Eccentric circles.
All at the same speed.
(Laughs.) Aristotle had his shortcomings.

God exists in change.
The rhythm of transformation.
Closer faster, farther slower.
Why? Why? Why?
Relationships.
Mars does not fit.

Break through, break through.
I am ready, I am ready.
Ask the question,
never be afraid to ask
Why?

What are the relationships over time?
How are we all linked?
every flower,
every rocky cliff,
circling together,
bound by the same laws,
laws for nature,
for man,
for the heavens.
God has placed an order
for us to see.
The brilliance of God's plan surrounds me.

I can't make it all fit.
I can't make them fit.
More numbers. I need more numbers.
Mars. Mars. Mars.
Why?

The Sister Upstairs

Robert Vivian

Scene: here and now

Dramatic
Pops: (50s) a fallen priest

> *Pops has been sharing a house with his daughter, Joan, and his two sisters, Boat and House. Over the years, Pops and Aunt Boat have overfed Aunt House to the point that she is no longer able to leave her bed. When Aunt Boat poisons her sister in an effort to end the poor woman's suffering, she and Pops must then confront their mutual culpability in House's condition. Boat encourages Pops to tell Joan about the sad demise of House and receives the following response.*

POPS: My whole life has been dominated by females. They won't leave me alone. It's like sex isn't even a part of me—it was just handed out like a party favor. My drive isn't in my pants. It's in my head. I'm a cerebral lover. You know that. I get off by thinking. What this means in rational terms I have no idea. I'm surrounded by grotesques. Before God as my witness, I'm screwed up. Right and wrong have been thrown in the frying pan with everything else. And you want me to make amends. Don't you think I want to? But Jesus Christ, I have no idea where to start. None of you give me a moment's peace to think the whole thing through. I'm too busy planning the next meal.

The Sister Upstairs

Robert Vivian

Scene: here and now

Dramatic
Pops: (50s) a fallen priest

> *His idealistic Joan-of-Arc-obsessed daughter has reacted poorly to the news of her aunt's death and has managed to shoot herself in the foot with her bow and arrow in a fit of pique. Here, miserable Pops bemoans his unhappy and unsavory life.*

POPS: *(Looking up the stairs.)* Hello up there. We have a lot to talk about.

(No response. The sound of rain.)

POPS: Don't clam up now. Aunt House is dead. Joan shot her own foot. I don't know how to operate a forklift, let alone move a mountain of flesh. *(Pause.)* I went for a walk. Do you hear me? I went around the city. I almost stepped on a cat that was long, thin, and wicked. Black ears. White feet. A foreigner in a distant land. *(Pause.)* I went into a drugstore. I came out. For no reason at all. I scanned the labels of booze with no intention of buying. That's the kind of state I'm in. Window shopping. I walked out. I kept going. Rain got in my eyes, down my neck, under the soles of my shoes. I stink. But I realized something out there. *We don't have to be here.* We can go away. We have freedom of movement. We're not tied to House anymore. Maybe Boat was right to poison her. House was a fine woman but a vulture at the end. I'm through pretending. Let's move on, shall we? We're not as corrupt as you think. And I'm ready to own up to a few things, my part in all this. Let me tell you a story. *(He gathers himself before speaking.)* Once I gave bad advice to a young couple about their baby. I told them to give it up. I told them they weren't fit parents when I knew all along they'd believe me. They trusted me. I told them to give it up because they weren't capable of real love. They believed me. I told them because they trusted me and I almost ended up believing it myself. And they did. They gave up the child and then split up themselves eight months later. All because I told them! *I* told them to do it and they listened! Because they were young and the husband liked to have a few beers on the weekend! But they were fine, they were gentle souls! He would have made a great dad and I knew it! *(Pause.)* He had something I didn't. He had grace. Well, what do you make of that? I abused my powers of persuasion. I went for their hearts and came up with blood on my shirt. Answer me, why don't you? Who's up there? *(Pause.)* I know Joan's foot is hurting. Christ, she shot herself in the foot. Come on down and we'll talk about it. No funny business. I'm through cooking. House is dead. Can't you see the dilemma here? She was fantastically obese. *(Pause.)* In a way I blame myself. I fed her. You just supplied the goods. So tell you what: we'll reach a bargain. We'll carry her out right now and dump her in the lake. All three of us. It won't be easy, but nothing worthwhile is. We'll weigh her down with rocks. We'll strap her to a car. I'm not trying to be morbid. I'm being practical for once. I loved her like a wife. But I'm not sure if we're fit for society, if we're not screwed up somehow, if our hearts are in the right place. I abused my powers of persuasion. People confided in me and I let 'em have it. I twisted the facts. I didn't have humility. I was a bad priest, a bad seed, a fair to middling cook. Forget my homemade sausage. I'm giving up spatulas forever. And the funny thing is, I don't even consider myself an evil guy! Just…a little lost.

Soda Fountain

Richard Lay

Scene: a small American town, summer, 1969

Serio-Comic
Danny: (20s) an alcoholic draft-dodger hopelessly in love with best friend's girl…who also happens to be his drinking partner

> *When Johnny shipped out for Vietnam he left his best friend and his fiancée behind to keep the home fires burning. Unfortunately, Both Danny and Sally soon turned to booze in an effort to cope with their fears and sense of ennui. Here, philosophical Danny reveals his love for Sally.*

DANNY: *(Chopping wood.)* There is nothing quite as sweet as the torment of un-requited love…reason flees, thoughts concentrate…When you love somebody and they don't love you back…you live on impossible hope. And that hope is your friend, food and drink…Then there's the real drink…so you drink to forget and all that does is make you remember more…Remember the things she said and the things you hoped she would say. Unrequited love is God's preview of Hell…That's my opinion, anyway…I see Sally about twice a month. We go for a drink after she closes the soda fountain. Sometimes we play pool, sometimes we just talk. On the outset the talk is chit-chat about ice cream and sodas…and the new grill she put in to make money on breakfast and lunch…then as we drink beer and put that Beatles stuff on the juke-box, I tell her I love her and she looks at me and says not in a million, billion, zillion fucking years would she ever consider me as ANYTHING. *(Smiles.)* But she says it with that lop-sided smile and her green eyes from heaven. It's the same every time we meet. Then she says things like "You want to have an affair, don't you?" So in my own defense, if that's what it is, I tell her I don't need her anyway. Then we part and then there's silence and then she calls me maybe a week later. Sometimes I pray that she will call me…and when she does I sound to myself like I'm talking through a wad of cotton wool. My voice sounds flat and I hear myself ending the conversation too soon…and I put the phone down—and my despair is doubled. But I ask you this, if she doesn't love me why would she bother to call me possessive? Anyway, Sally is the sweetheart of Vietnam war hero Johnny Green…Johnny the war hero. Who'd have thought it. We grew up together. He was shy and I was sorta wild. I chased the girls…and he tagged along. I lead and he followed. I was on the high school football team and Johnny was the star of the chess club…We grew up together. I boxed on the college team—oh yeah we were at college together—and he was president of the Scandinavian Poets Society. As our interests outgrew our friendship it came down to one common denominator…we both loved Sally. Then came what they called a war. In Vietnam…WHERE WAS VIETNAM ON THE MAP? Johnny was one of the first in this town to enlist. He believed all that crap about the Communists and the domino theory and the threat to the Western World. I thought about it and listened to Jane Fonda and I burned the flag and smoked pot and protested and before I knew it I had dodged the draft. I said I wanted to be a Catholic priest. That was enough to keep me out of Nam…Then it started…I don't know what you'd call it. Self-doubt. Self-disgust, coward, cowardly action. My mind was talking and I wasn't listening. I was hearing all sorts of things…things like only black guys were being sent into action; things like Johnson and Nixon were Communist agents. Things like America shouldn't get involved…Things like the REAL heroes were the ones who didn't go. I admired Muhammed Ali. And in the very forefront of my mind, my thoughts, my everything, was my desire to win Sally's affections…But I got it wrong, didn't I? She loved HIM. She loves HIM…Well, today he's back with a big medal pinned to his scrawny chest…don't mistake my anger…I love Johnny…we are only enemies in love with the same woman. I want Sally. She wants Johnny…We'll see…I hope she hides her bottles…I just hope.

Soda Fountain

Richard Lay

Scene: a small American town, summer, 1969

Serio-Comic
Danny: (20s) an alcoholic draft-dodger hopelessly in love with best friend's girl…who also happens to be his drinking partner

> *When Johnny returns home from Vietnam a hero, he finds his fiancée and best friend have turned into drunks. Here, Danny reflects on Johnny's homecoming.*

DANNY: *(To audience.)* That's Sally with her shouting bottle. The joke is that Johnny has no idea she is drunkard than a rat before noon. There's no reason he should. She just took to it and you can't blame it on anybody. In an ideal world you would blame it on Johnny going to Vietnam. No, it wasn't that. No, no, no, it was a chemical thing…One day she was running the Soda Fountain, nice as pie…and the next thing is that she is married to Jack Daniels.

[FROGGY: *(Sleepily.)* Worried about Sally?

DANNY: Once I said to Sally that I would fulfill her biggest dream and help her start up a horse farm with fine stables and leather smelling like life itself. There would be everything she ever wanted…When I told her she looked at me with more intensity than I had ever seen…she seemed on the brink of tears and she just kept LOOKING at me. I don't know if I saw a tear…but I felt something pretty important…like maybe she CARED…that she cared for ME. *(Smiles.)* She probably don't…but that's OK cos I got a few fields and a coupla' good barns and she could teach her ass off and not be drinking her wonderful life away. That would suit me…She just looked at me and screwed her nose up and put her tongue on her top teeth and sort of pouted…the way she has pouted since even before I fell in love with her. So

112

anyway, I can't forget the look she gave me...her wonderful green eyes and set lips verging on a smile. Not to mention her come hither grin crumbling into a cigarette chuckle as you might find in a Oklahoma City pool hall on a wet Sunday afternoon from a woman who hadn't been to church. Her Ma's coming home from Galvaston any minute. She's always liked me—she says I have manners. She says I have grace, whatever that means.

Soul Survivor

Ted Lange

Scene: here and now

Serio-Comic
Guy: (30s) An African American Everyman with a good eye for detail

> *Guy's day begins with a visit from the Devil, whose offer of temptation the sharp-eyed mailman rejects. Later that same day, Guy meets the woman of his dreams and sees the route to true happiness. Perhaps the confluence of such cosmic forces have made to him a gift of insight or perhaps he had it all along. In any case, Guy here shares a canny observation of the general personality of the young white power elite.*

GUY: When I was in high school, I used to hang out with all the white boys. Through me, they became hip. They knew about the Beach Boys. I knew about Smokey Robinson and the Miracles. They knew about Penny Loafers, I knew about the power handshake. We exchanged ideas and talked about how the people in power had screwed up this world. How their fathers kept my father down. How a brighter day would come when we would walk arm and arm, and right the wrongs of this world. We marched together, sat in together, protested together. We worked on changing this world. But now I can't find them anymore. All the hip white boys are gone. It's like they sold their souls to the devil. Oh, occasionally, you'll see a hip white boy blowing a horn or strumming a guitar. Every now and then, one pops up with a book or stops you at a dinner party. But the guys in power, the guys who have finally arrived at a position to change things, don't! They've become their fathers with one small difference. They're hip. They screw you in a hip way. They can recite every hit Smokey ever had and screw you at the same time. They've sold their souls like their fathers, and I helped to educate them on how to do us in, with style.

Stars

Romulus Linney

Scene: Manhattan, a penthouse terrace on a summer night

Serio-Comic
He: (30s–40)

> *While at a party featuring Manhattan's hoi polloi, our hero tells a woman he's just met the story of how he first got together with his wife.*

HE: *(Pause.)* I'm in a bar on Columbus Avenue. I meet a woman who says she's a schoolteacher. We have fun, a really good time. She takes me home. It's good. I leave about eleven, she's looking at me like I'm an angel from heaven. Four o'clock in the morning, my telephone rings. It's her, sounding terrible. Help! Right now! So I go back to her apartment and she is looking at me like I'm a demon from hell. "What's the matter?" "Did you call me on the phone?" "When?" "Right after you went home." "No." "You swear?" "I swear." "Oh, my God, my God!" "What happened?" I said. "What a *fool* I am! What a fool I am!" she said. *"What happened?"* "Well," she said, "about eleven thirty a man whose voice sounded I thought just like yours called me. You, I thought it was you, said you had a way of making us both some money right now but you needed two hundred dollars first, and didn't have any cash, did I? Yes. Would I lend it to you. Oh, I had such a good time with you, I liked you so much, so I said yes, I have that, come get it. You, I thought it was you, said, no, you wanted me to meet a man and give it to him, with whatever else he asked for. "What?" I said. You told me to go to a children's playground off Central Park West at midnight, and just sit in a swing and wait. You hoped I would do this for you. I was speechless, and God help me, I was excited. I got the money and went. There were shadows of people at the playground, coming and going in darkness, there for sex. I was frightened and disgusted with myself and terribly, terribly alive. He was wearing a cowboy hat. When he came up to me and when I saw it wasn't you, I was horrified and thrilled. I gave him two hundred dollars and he pulled on his belt and I knelt down and gave him sex. He thanked me and was gone, leaving me there on my knees. I felt—well—debased but delivered. Then I thought, was that really like you? What if it wasn't you who called me? Was it? Oh, tell me the truth! We did meet in a bar but you were decent, weren't you? You wouldn't do that to me, would you? But who else could have? Nobody knew about us. It has to be you! "No it doesn't," I said. "It could be somebody in the bar." "Oh," she said. "But I don't go there often. I don't!" "Sometimes?" "Well, yes." She thought a minute. That man, with the cowboy hat, he could have heard us, heard I was taking you home." "Right." "But that means it was somebody who knows me, my phone number, and everything." "That's the only other possibility." "Oh, God," she said. "I don't know what to believe. Was it some man who's been watching me in that bar? Or was it you? Who did that to me?"

[SHE: Do you expect me to believe this?]

HE: It's true.

Sticky and Shary

Rob Handel

Scene: NYC

Serio-Comic
Sticky: a teenaged ghost

> *Sticky was accidentally killed when he slipped and fell on the bathroom floor when his sister, Shary committed suicide. Here, the wandering spirit shares a memory of an evening at home with his family before everything was lost.*

STICKY: So my mom's dating this guy with violet hair. Not even purple—violet. And Mom explains that Zach is a performance artist, which means we have to shlep down to Avenue B at ten p.m. Friday night and watch him do stuff in front of five people in a damp basement with black walls. Thing turns out to be a three-hour epic called "I Hate My Life And Now You Can Too." It's absolutely the most boring time of my entire life; I could only compare it to Remote Control Weekend on MTV. There's one part that's okay, where Zach plays this cool teenager who tortures small animals so that's kinda funny, but basically I'd rather watch a landfill. We take the subway back uptown, shrewd move Mom, it's only two a.m. and you're dressed like the Shangri-Las on speed. Zach keeps saying "I'm on a performance high" which I guess means he wouldn't *normally* be feeling up my mom on the six train. I can spell out the rest of the night anyway: four a.m. I'll be tanning under the bedside lamp rereading the last six months of X-Men because mom and Zach are screwing too loud to sleep. I get another coke from the kitchen and I see my sister's college applications all over the living room floor and then I notice she's out by the window in her panties letting the wind hit her and I'm like "oh, great." But I'm so bored that I go over and ask her how it's going and stuff, and she just goes "Hi, Sticky" in this little voice and tells me I should be asleep, so I tell her if she's cool enough to stay up and be miserable then I'm twice as cool, and she thinks I'm funny, which is not very usual. I ask her if she wants a t-shirt or a Dristan or something but she just takes a sip of my coke. I don't know, we talk like about the college thing and I tell her I'm gonna die before I get that old or take off in a Porsche maybe. Actually, for my sister, she looks pretty happy. So it's one of those weird nights. She tells me I'm okay, and I tell her she has pretty good tits and I take the coke to my room.

Three Days of Rain

Richard Greenberg

Scene: NYC, 1995

Serio-Comic
Pip: (20–30) the son of a world-famous architect, an aspiring actor

Here, Pip describes his parents' first meeting and his mother's current state.

PIP: *(Solo.)* Hi. Hello. Okay: Now me. My name is Phillip O'Malley Wexler—well, Pip to those who've known me a little too long. My father, the architect Theodore Wexler, died of lung cancer at the age of thirty-eight, even though he was the only one of his generation who never smoked. I was three when it happened. So, of course, I forgot him instantly. My mother tried to make up for this by obsessively telling me stories about him, this kind of rolling epic that trailed me through life, but they, or it, ended up being mostly about her. Which was probably for the best. Anyway, it went like this: My mother, Maureen O'Malley back then, came to New York in the spring of '59. She was twenty, her parents staked her to a year, and she arrived with a carefully-thought-out plan to be amazing at something. Well, the year went by without much happening and she was miserable because she was afraid she was going to have to leave New York and return, in disgrace, to Brooklyn. Early one morning, after a night when she couldn't sleep at all, she started just wandering around the city. It was raining, she had her umbrella, she sat in the rain under her umbrella on a bench in Washington Square Park, and felt sorry for herself. Then she saw my father for the first time. "There he was," she told me, "this devastatingly handsome man"—that was an exaggeration, he looked like me—and he was obviously, miraculously, even *more* unhappy than she was. He was just

119

thrashing through the rain, pacing and thrashing, until, all at once, he stopped and sank onto the bench beside her. But not because of her. He didn't realize she was there. He didn't have an umbrella so my mother shifted hers over to him. "Despair," my mother told me, "can be attractive in a young person. Despair in a young person can be seductive." Well, eventually she got tired of him not noticing the wonderful thing she was doing for him so she said, a little too loudly: "Can I help you? May I be of help to you?" Because he'd been crying. And he jumped! Man, he *shrieked!* But he stayed anyway, and they talked, and I was born, the end. Okay. So, my mother had been telling me that story for about ten years before it occurred to me to ask: "Why was he crying? What was my father so upset about the first time he met you?" "I never knew," she said. He just told her he was fine, she took him to breakfast, they talked about nothing, and I guess she kind of gawked at him. And the more she gawked, I guess the happier he felt, because by the end of breakfast it was as if nothing had happened and they were laughing and my mother was in love and the worst day of her life had become the best day of her life. When she first came to New York, my mother would stay up till dawn debating Abstract Expressionism and "Krapp's Last Tape," and then she'd sneak out to a matinee of one of those plays you could never remember the plot of where the girl got caught in the rain and had to put on the man's bathrobe and they sort of did a little dance around each other and fell in love. And there wasn't even a single good joke, but my mother would walk out after and the city seemed dizzy with this absolutely random happiness, and that's how she met my father. She's hardly ever home any more. She travels from city to city. I think she's looking for another park bench, and another wet guy. That's okay. I hope she finds him.

To Each His Own
(Dead and Gone To Granny's)
Jussi Wahlgren

Scene: a garage in a large family home in suburban Finland

Dramatic
Patrick: (36) a man who has lost everything that mattered to him in one day

> *Patrick plans on committing suicide. When his first effort is interrupted by the arrival of his younger brother, the two men find themselves sharing bittersweet memories of their childhood.*

PATRICK: I was better than you in ice skating, pool, crazy golf, table tennis…Do you remember the summers when we visited granny at Lake Eno. I hated when we went berry picking with the colonel, the branches tore my arms and I got bitten to shit by the mosquitoes. And the old man kept a watch on me so that I wouldn't eat one single berry.

[FREDDIE: Some times granny would join us, and mother and aunt-Hilda too.]

PATRICK: Granny used to let me just sit on a log while she picked the blue berries all around me and told stories about the fairies in the forest. The old man saw that I wasn't picking. He would draw himself to attention three feet away from me, looking me straight in the eye—I would calmly eat the berries—and he would say: "Carry on, boy!" and his face would turn red and he'd march off. Granny would wink at me and continue telling her fairy tales. I enjoyed the power she had over the colonel…

[FREDDIE: And granny's wild berry fool!]

PATRICK: Back on the farm we sat on the warm stone steps of the old barn, the sun was shining and butterflies fluttered in the meadow. God. I was a lucky little bugger then.

Unpacking Dominic's Trunk

Terryl Paiste

Scene: the Twinkle Toes Dance Studio, Peoria, IL, 1984

Dramatic
Dominic: (60s) a retired accountant

> *Dominic has recently moved-in with his divorced niece,
> Kendall, who runs her own dance studio. It becomes quite
> obvious that these two will have to go through a period of
> adjustment before settling in to a life together. Here, Dominic
> helps things along when he tells Kendall the story of her
> birth.*

DOMINIC: You remember how I told you once that when I got out
of the army, I didn't much care what I went to school for? That
the important thing was to use the G.I. Bill to get a degree, any
degree, so I could make a decent living and support a family?

   [KENDALL: I remember. And I'm sorry the right woman didn't
   have the good sense to snap you up.]

DOMINIC: That's only half of it. The thing is, I always had this feeling that there was someone out there waiting to be born, *my* kid.
And this kid was tired of waiting, impatient, you know? Anyway,
when I got the call that your mother had given birth to you, I didn't
want to go visit her in the hospital. I'd made that trip for seven
nieces and three nephews by that time, and with each one I felt
more and more cheated. It seemed like everybody else in the family, everybody else in the world was having their kid, where the
hell was mine? *(Paces.)* So I kept putting off going to the hospital, and finally it was the evening before your mother was supposed to go home—they used to keep women in the hospital a
sensible amount of time then, not like today where they wheel
you straight out of the delivery room and into the nearest taxi—
and I'd run out of excuses. So I drove to the hospital in the mid-

dle of a thunderstorm, thinking, "Serves you right for putting it off, you stupid bastard," and planning how I'd grab a box of candy in the gift shop and be done with the whole thing in fifteen minutes or less. But when I got to your mother's room, your father and the other visitors had already come and gone, and your mother was lying there sound asleep with you in her arms.

[KENDALL: *(Fascinated.)* How come you never told me this story before?]

DOMINIC: You were lying there as calm as can be and without thinking what I was doing, I picked you up and carried you over to the window. The storm was putting on quite a show—thunder, lightning, the works. Now, there's not a whole lot of conversation you can carry on with a three-day-old baby, but I thought you might be interested in where thunder comes from and what lightning is all about, so I told you. And you listened. I swear to God, as we stood by that window, you understood every word I was saying. I know infants are supposed to be afraid of bright lights and noise, but your eyes were wide open and you weren't afraid at all. No, you were impressed. Impressed with the lightning, impressed with— *(Stops and looks away for a second, embarrassed, then looks back at her and continues.)* With me. I think maybe you got the idea that I was somehow responsible for what you were seeing, that maybe I *caused* the lightning, and all for your amusement.

[KENDALL: Well, maybe you did.]

DOMINIC: And here's the weird part. After I woke up your mother and was driving back home, I knew that I was never gonna be bothered by that nagging, unborn child again. That she had made it into the world after all, without any help from me, and that regardless of who the mother was or the father...you were mine. *(Shrugs.)* Stupid, isn't it?

War Monologue

Tom Greenwell

Scene: Great Britain—there and now

Dramatic
A retired British soldier: (60s)

Here, a soldier remembers his experiences in World War II.

SOLDIER: What on earth are you talking about? Why should you feel guilty just because you weren't in the armed forces in the war? You were in London, weren't you? In the Blitz, too. My God! I couldn't have coped with that. Oh yes. I was on Malta convoys all right. Scared half to death by those Stuka dive bombers too. But it was always the same for me. After a week or two at sea I'd be back in dear old Alexandria living it up. No ration books. No blackout. Of *course* I had a lucky war. But like everybody else I went where I was sent and did what I was told. What I remember most about it is that if I'd had the courage I would probably have been a coward several times over. The fact that I wasn't, at any rate outwardly, was due to my being more afraid of what my colleagues and my macho dad would think of me than I was of anything else. Anyway, how far can you run when you're on a bloody ship? What was that? Oh of course. Well, when things got especially nasty I used to comfort myself with the thought that at least I wasn't in the poor bloody infantry, bayonet at the ready, or pinned down in some stinking trench with bodies piling up ever higher and higher. And I wasn't a Desert Rat struggling to get away from a blazing tank only to be finished off by a burst of machine-gun fire as soon as he'd hit the sand.

And I wasn't, thank God, one of those kid RAF pilots back home with a fifty-fifty chance several times a day of ending up either dead or horribly deformed. And I wasn't escorting Russian convoys, where the freezing cold would probably have done for me even if the enemy hadn't. Nor was I a POW in a Jap horror camp. And I wasn't a merchant seaman, running all the risks without a chance to hit back and no hope of getting a string of medals to leave to a grieving family. And anyway, I kept asking myself, could anything be more grim and terrifying than the plight of the Jews in Nazi Germany and occupied Europe, and the dreadful wanderings and deprivations of refugees and divided families all over the stricken Continent? Memory tells me that even when I was being torpedoed and dive-bombed I usually managed to persuade myself that I was bloody lucky to be where I was and not somewhere even worse….Yes, well…I'm still here, aren't I? I don't want to sound pompous, but it's a common feature of wartime experiences that many survivors of an action which has claimed the lives of friends and colleagues feel guilty at having come through it. Although from time to time I shared that unease I always managed to get over it. After all, there was still a war on, and how was I to know that it wouldn't be my turn tomorrow or next week?

Yes; most of us had a hang-up of one sort or another. Some chaps I knew couldn't stand the strain of being lucky. One of them, a telegraphist whom I only remember as "Scouse," had been granted a transfer from his ship just before she set sail on what was destined to be her last voyage. Four survivors, I believe…He spent the rest of his war volunteering for hazardous jobs in Combined Operations. I bumped into him a few times and he always sounded like a man who felt himself doomed to spend the rest of his life being dogged by rotten good fortune.…Then one day I heard that he'd found peace at last when he was blown up on an Italian invasion beach. No, I'm not quite finished yet. What had become my theme song, "How lucky I was not to be…" got another cue on VE Day. Because of a long-standing engagement I was at the Houses of Parliament and happened to be in the main lobby when Churchill came through on his way to join the King and Queen. It was a very emotional moment and I thought to myself: However grim the war might have been for the rest of us, and still was for the poor devils in the Far East, how lucky we were not to have been him, with all that awesome decision-making; with all that frightening knowledge and understanding of what the real odds were against us after the fall of France, and when the U-Boats were still winning the Battle of the Atlantic. God Bless the old bugger! No; I didn't get anything special. Only the usual campaign medals for being in the right war zones at the right time. I suppose I'm quite proud of them really. But you know, many thousands of men and women who got fewer ribbons than I did never lived to wear them.

Wedding Dance

Dominic A. Taylor

Scene: a wedding reception in Chicago

Dramatic
Milton: (20–30) a man who is slightly retarded

> *Here, Milton places centerpieces and place cards on the*
> *tables at a friend's wedding reception and reveals his keen*
> *sense of logic.*

MILTON: A place for everyone, and everyone has a place. A place for every one. Every one has a place. A place for everyone, and everyone has someone. A place for a person, and everyone for someone. A person for a person if they are in the right place. They can dance. Rhythm aint no problem in dancing. Rhythm is a problem in dancing good. Aint nothing in dancing but trying. If you got some music you gotta just try. A place for everyone, and everyone has a place. If you don't get the tags in the right place, people won't know where to go. If people don't know where to sit, they will have no idea how to stand up. Isn't that right Milton? Well of course that's right. And that's why they gave you this job. A very important job. Because without it we would have a problem. People not knowing where to sit? Problem. Like trying to earn a dollar and find love. A place for every one. Every one has a place. A place for everyone, and everyone has someone. A place for a person, and everyone for someone. A person for a person if they are in the right place. Those are two full time jobs. Earning and loving. And you only get your benefits after the probation period. People come to a wedding, they receive the bride and groom with no place to sit. Or without the right place to sit. They just won't know nothing. Then their next question, when to get up? But you gotta be seated first. You gotta have the right seat. That's my job. But I'm lucky cause I have charts, and myths, and I have learned some things. Where things go. A place for every one. Every one has a place. A place for everyone, and everyone has someone. A place for a person, and everyone for someone. A person for a person if they are in the right place. So putting people in the right place is an important job. Done wrong, a problem. Done correct we can still have problems. Just less problems, problems start with things being out of place. Every time I been in trouble it's because I was at the wrong place at the wrong time. Which happens. Being at a wedding, it's all under schedule. Or on a schedule. So Like I said, it's just about being in the right place. Wrong place, wrong time cuts short things. Right place, right time hugs and kisses, dancing and bliss. A place for every one. Every one has a place. A place for everyone, and everyone has someone. A place for a person, and everyone for someone. A person for a person if they are in the right place.

We Make a Wall

Gary Garrison

Scene: Bensonhurst, Brooklyn

Serio-Comic
Marty the Mover: (30s–40s) a philosophical mover

> *Marty has been hired to empty out Benny's house by Angie,*
> *Benny's unhappy wife. When Benny furiously demands to*
> *know where Angie has gone, Marty does his best to offer a*
> *bit of calming insight.*

MARTY: *(Starts folding his table.)* I got a heart for people like you
about as big as this room, you know? But I got no patience for
you. How could you live life this long and know nothin' about
livin' it *right?* My old lady would look at you and say, "Patience,
Marty, he just hasn't gotten his wake up call yet."

[BENNY: And you have?]

MARTY: *(Folding the chairs.)* You damn right. Let me tell you a little story, chump, I come home one day. And my youngest,
Theresa, is sitting on the stairs waitin' for me. I come in the door
and kiss her on the cheek—she wipes it off. I kiss her again. She
wipes it off and frowns—the little shit. I take her head in almost
a bear-lock, and plant the loudest, sloppiest, wettest kiss on her
forehead these two lips could muster. She wipes it off with one
hand, then the other, then scrapes the walls with her hands. I'm
about ready to pop her one, 'cause I'm good and—you know,
hurt. And she looks up with those big bright blue eyes and says:
"Pop-o, I told you, no more kisses 'till you apologize."
"Apologize for what?!", I said. Then there was this silence—the
longest moment of my life, I tell you. I'm lookin' at her, she's
lookin at me—we got thirty years between us and I feel like a
friggin' baby next to her. But I can't remember nothin'. And I
don't want to guess and make it all worse. And my mind's racing,

and she's just starin' at me, drillin' a hole right through me. I can't think of nothin. What was it? WHAT WAS IT? Why can't I remember what I did that I should apologize for? And I ain't a good actor, you know? So she knows I forgot. And she turns and goes upstairs. And I'm still standin' there, sweatin'—almost cryin', man, 'cause I know I let her down.

[BENNY: My heart's bleedin', Marty, bleedin'. Who cares?!]

MARTY: Don't you get it? It wasn't about what I did or didn't do to her, what I forgot or didn't forget—the fact is, I'm BIGGER than she is. And when you're bigger than someone, you can DO ANYTHING, BE anything, and SAY anything…I mean, who's gonna question you?…Somebody who loves you, if you're lucky. *(He walks towards the door.)* This is your wake-up call, pal. Try not to blow it.

What Cats Know

Lisa Dillman

Scene: Chicago

Serio-Comic
Kent: (30s) a man struggling to make a relationship work

> *Kent has learned the hard way that it takes a lot of work to keep a marriage afloat. Here he describes the rather painful demise of his first marriage.*

KENT: [Erin. She's twelve now. She's a good kid.] *(Beat.)* When Maggie left me, she just got up one morning, made the coffee, and while I was drinking it, she told me that she couldn't stand me. She said she hated every single thing about me. Just like that.

[Gregory stops sketching a moment.]

KENT: I'm thick. In four years, I had never once thought, Hey, am I a jerk? Now I ask myself that question all the time.

[GREGORY: And what does your self answer?]

KENT: He pretty much tells me I'm okay. *(Beat.)* After Maggie kicked me out, I moved to a little dark pit of a room with moss-green shag carpeting. I quit my job and I spent days and nights just lying on that carpet, staring at the ceiling cracks. There was one that looked just like Jackie Gleason in profile. I didn't change my clothes for a week at a time. *(Beat.)* I was like that for a month. Then one day, a little spot of sunshine came through one of the blinds. It hit the floor next to my head…and it was really *warm*. I got up and opened the window. And there was a cat sitting there. On the window ledge. I don't know where the hell he came from; I mean, I lived on the third floor. But when I opened that window, he just strolled in. Harold. What a bunged up guy he was. His ears were in shreds. He was a tough cat.

[GREGORY: What happened to him?]

KENT: Oh, he stayed with me in that apartment for a while. I got myself up off the floor. I got another job and a hide-a-bed. I called Maggie and told her I needed a picture of the three of us—me, Maggie, and Erin. She knew the one I wanted. It was taken in our backyard in Toledo. Really green and there were big purple lilacs behind us. We looked really young. Good. We looked good. She sent me the picture the next week. Only thing is, she cut herself out. With an X-acto. Very...surgical job. There I was with Erin and then this outline of Maggie. Like a ghost. It turned out she'd been sleeping with an old college buddy of mine for a couple of years. *(Beat.)* Anyway. I moved to Chicago. With Harold. I met Cass. Three days after Cass moved in, Harold moved out.

What Cats Know

Lisa Dillman

Scene: Chicago

Serio-Comic
Gregory: (30s) an artist

> *Gregory and Cass sleep together when Cass's partner, Kent, is away on business. When Cass subsequently announces that she and Kent are expecting a baby, Gregory makes the following overly gushing response to the news.*

GREGORY: Especially both of you. Procreation! I just think that takes so much guts these days.

[KENT: Or forgetfulness.]

[CASS: Kent. *(She punches him again.)*]

[THERESE: God, you're like a couple of *puppies.*]

GREGORY: But you know what I mean? The world's full of all this rotten, putrid stuff and it's getting worse with every nanosecond that ticks by. Every jiffy taking us into this uncertain future. Uncertain, but I mean the prospects do not look good. And then you figure, I mean, face it, by the time your little guy is college age, hell, his parents could be *homeless.* I mean, just because the potential is there for all of us to be living on the street if we have even a *little* bad luck. And then I think of how messed up my parents were and I figure, you know, that everyone's parents were messed up in *lots* of ways—my parents weren't even special in that regard. And it must be incredibly easy to imprint yourself on your kid genetically and then back up all your misinformation when the little tike finally pokes his nose out into the wide world. And you try and try not to repeat what you feel were your parents' mistakes—but, you see, you don't even *have* to because there are brand-*new* mistakes to be made. The ones your children's generation will write about. Anyway, I think it's great. Reminds me of the pioneers. *(Toasts.)* To the pioneers.

   (Beat; all raise glasses. Blackout.)

When a Diva Dreams

Gary Garrison

Scene: Diva's, a cabaret in New Orleans

Dramatic
Lipton: (60s) a man doing his best to help a friend in need

> *Lipton has worked for many years for Miss Rose at Diva's.*
> *When lack of funds threatens to close the cabaret, all is dire*
> *until Miss Rose's sister, Delle, shows up out of the blue with*
> *enough money to keep Diva's afloat. Taking the money from*
> *the sister who walked out on her family and broke her*
> *father's heart presents an ethical dilemma for Miss Rose.*
> *Here, sage Lipton shares advice and wisdom with his old*
> *friend.*

LIPTON: *(Warmly.)* I didn't go to the store, Miss Red. Couldn't think of leavin' you when…when I knew that woman was here and chances were good she'd do a little damage.

[MISS RED: *(Softly.)* Not a little.]

LIPTON: Well, I thought as much. There's nothin' tender 'bout that woman, and when someone walks through your life with no trace of tenderness, people are gonna get hurt. And if you're family, you're gonna get hurt bad, 'cause family is the spoon that stirs your pot like nobody else.

[MISS RED: *(Quietly.)* Amen.]

LIPTON: I had a old hound dog, Miss Red. His name was Buster. Loved that dog like a wife. Anyway, one early morning me and old Buster was down at Coleman's Gully fishing for Buster's favorite: crawdads. Never knew a dog to eat shellfish, but Buster could make his way through a pound and a half of shrimp or crawfish 'for he'd stop. Well, we were having a good day that day. I bet I caught five pounds of crawfish 'for the sun broke over the horizon. Old Buster was a lickin' his chops and waggin' that tale ninety-miles an hour. He knew there was a feast in that bucket. Now for some reason, on this particular morning, Buster wasn't in a sharin' mood. He wanted every one of them crawfish. Everytime I reached for the bucket, he'd snarl and snap at me. What was I to do? So I let him have it—the whole bucket. And he ate every crawfish in there, that tale just a waggin'. He died about an hour later…Some family's are like that. They're greedy, and they'll take everything you offer them and you'll always give them everything you got. But sooner or later, someone's gonna croak on the excess. *(He starts to exit, then turns back.)* Don't give her everything you got. It's the best thing for both of you.

Whiteout

Jocelyn Beard

Scene: the home of John Creek, a white separatist and militia leader, Idaho

Dramatic
Senator Dan Tattinger: (60) An African American man trapped behind enemy lines and fighting to save the life of his illegitimate daughter

> *The Senator's private plane has crashed in a blizzard on mountain property belonging to John Creek, the racist leader of the country's largest private militia. The plane was carrying Dan's racially-mixed daughter, public knowledge of whose existence could ruin his political future. Dan's wife, Rebecca, is a proud African American woman who has made issues of race her only political concerns. Here, a frustrated Dan finally explodes when she confronts him with the fact that she is furious because his illegitimate daughter is half-white.*

DAN: [No, you're not.] The power of politics has changed you, Rebecca. It's given you tunnel vision.

[REBECCA: What??]

DAN: You see things only in terms of black versus white. Us against them.

[REBECCA: That's the way it is!]

DAN: It isn't! Lunatics like Farrakhan will have you believe such a simplistic lie, but the fact is, Rebecca, that racism in America is doomed. Watch the talk shows, for chrissakes!

[REBECCA: You're insane!]

DAN: And you've become rarefied. Your involvement with virtually every political organization dedicated to the black cause has hypnotized you into thinking it's the *only* cause. You're as bad as the right-to-lifers! Watch the goddamn talk shows! That's where you see America in all its glory. White girls having black boys' babies. Black girls having white boys' babies. Girls, Rebecca—not women. Color is moot. A ruined life has no color and America knows this! Watch the talk shows! Media-saturated white suburban teenagers dressed like urban blacks droning on and on about how we should all be "colorblind." Oprah parading her politically correct racially mixed group of cronies before millions and millions of black and white devotees daily. Black and white LA gangsta girls raising their mixed-race babies to be gang members, side by side. Side by side, Rebecca. *That* is what America wants. America wants health care reform, tax forms that make sense, social security to keep paying into the next millennium, corporations to stop behaving like pirates sailing along the Spanish Main, child care that doesn't cost a month's salary and most importantly, America wants a kick-ass education system that will produce kids who can rule the world and someday the stars. The stars, Rebecca. Do you think that anyone will give a flying hello if the first person to pilot a rocket to Mars is black, white, red or female? America just wants to get there, we don't care who drives the car! America just wants to survive long enough to see the future we promised the kids in the 50s and the 60s. America *doesn't* want our public school curriculum to be changed to include "African" studies. America doesn't want Ebonics. America doesn't want Affirmative Action. America doesn't want anything that *you* want, Rebecca. You're a dinosaur. You're as out of touch with reality as Creek. Both of you are trapped in the past. Only in your case it's unforgivable because the past you're trapped in doesn't even belong to you; it belongs to your great-grandmother, and she's dead. She gave you that necklace so you would never forget where you came from, not to use as a talisman for a new world order. Look at you. You're *still* all dressed up with no place to go.

Permissions Acknowledgments

NOTE: These monologues are intended to be used for audition and class study; permission is not required to use the material for those purposes. However, if there is a paid performance of any of the monologues included in this book, please refer to these permissions acknowledgment pages to locate the source who can grant permission for public performance.

Alki Copyright © 1997 by Eric Overmeyer. Reprinted by permission of William Morris Agency. CAUTION: Professionals and amateurs are hereby warned that performance of *Alki* by Eric Overmeyer is subject to royalty. It is fully protected under the copyright laws of the United States of America, and of all countries covered by the International Copyright Union (including the Dominion of Canada and the rest of the British Commonwealth), and of all countries covered by the Pan-American Copyright Convention and the Universal Copyright Convention, the Berne Convention and of all countries with which the United States has reciprocal copyright relations. All rights, including professional, amateur/motion picture stage rights, recitation, lecturing, public reading, radio broadcasting, television, video or sound recording, all other forms of mechanical or electronic reproduction, such as CD-ROM, CD-1, information storage and retrieval systems and photocopying, and the rights of translation into foreign languages, are strictly reserved. Particular emphasis is laid upon the matter of readings, permission for which must be obtained from the author's agent in writing. Contact: William Morris Agency, 1325 Avenue of the Americas, New York, NY 10019, Attn: George Lane, Author's Agent

Autumn Canticle Copyright © 1997 by John W. Lowell. Reprinted by permission of the author. CAUTION: Professionals and amateurs are hereby warned that performance of *Autumn Canticle* by John W. Lowell is subject to royalty. It is fully protected under the copyright laws of the United States of America, and of all countries covered by the International Copyright Union (including the Dominion of Canada and the rest of the British Commonwealth), and of all countries covered by the Pan-American Copyright Convention and the Universal Copyright Convention, the Berne Convention and of all countries with which the United States has reciprocal copyright relations. All rights, including professional, amateur/motion picture stage rights, recitation, lecturing, public reading, radio broadcasting, television, video or sound recording, all other forms of mechanical or electronic reproduction, such as CD-ROM, CD-1, information storage and retrieval systems and photocopying, and the rights of translation into foreign languages, are strictly reserved. Particular emphasis is laid upon the matter of readings, permission for which must be obtained from the author's agent in writing. Contact: Harden-Curtis Associates, 850 7th Avenue, Suite 405, New York, NY 10019, Attn: Robert Kohn, Author's Agent

Bafo Copyright © 1997 by Tom Strelich. Reprinted by permission of Berman, Boals & Flynn. CAUTION: Professionals and amateurs are hereby warned that performance of *Bafo* by

Tom Strelich is subject to royalty. It is fully protected under the copyright laws of the United States of America, and of all countries covered by the International Copyright Union (including the Dominion of Canada and the rest of the British Commonwealth), and of all countries covered by the Pan-American Copyright Convention and the Universal Copyright Convention, the Berne Convention and of all countries with which the United States has reciprocal copyright relations. All rights, including professional, amateur/motion picture stage rights, recitation, lecturing, public reading, radio broadcasting, television, video or sound recording, all other forms of mechanical or electronic reproduction, such as CD-ROM, CD-1, information storage and retrieval systems and photocopying, and the rights of translation into foreign languages, are strictly reserved. Particular emphasis is laid upon the matter of readings, permission for which must be obtained from the author's agent in writing. Contact: Berman, Boals & Flynn

A Body Not Greatly Changed Copyright © 1997 by Jo J. Adamson. Reprinted by permission of the author. Contact: Jo J. Adamson, 25252 Lake Wilderness, Coun, Maple Valley, WA

By The Sea. By The Sea, By The Beautiful Sea: "Dawn" Copyright © 1996 by Joe Pintauro. CAUTION: The reprinting of *Dawn* included in this volume is reprinted by permission of the author and Dramatists Play Service, Inc., 440 Park Avenue South, New York, NY 10016. No professional or non-professional production of the play may be given without obtaining, in advance, the written permission of Dramatists Play Service, Inc., and paying the requisite fee. Inquiries regarding all other rights should be addressed to: Gilbert Parker, William Morris Agency, 1325 Avenue of the Americas, New York, NY 10019

By The Sea, By The Sea, By The Beautiful Sea: "Dusk" Copyright © 1996 by Terrence McNally. CAUTION: The reprinting of *Dusk* included in this volume is reprinted by permission of the author and Dramatists Play Service, Inc., 440 Park Avenue South, New York, NY 10016. No professional or non-professional production of the play may be given without obtaining, in advance, the written permission of Dramatists Play Service, Inc., and paying the requisite fee. Inquiries regarding all other rights should be addressed to: Gilbert Parker, William Morris Agency, 1325 Avenue of the Americas, New York, NY 10019

Carpool Copyright © 1997 by Laura Hembree. Reprinted by permission of Rosenstone/ Wender. Contact: Rosenstone/Wender, 3 East 48th Street, New York, NY 10017, (212) 832-8330, Attn: Ronald Gwiazda, Author's Agent

City Boy In A Cowboy Town Copyright © 1997 by Mark Leiren-Young. Reprinted by permission of the author. Contact: Playwrights' Union of Canada, 54 Wolseley Street, 2nd Floor, Toronto, Ontario M5T IA5, Canada

The Confession Of Many Strangers Copyright © 1997 by Lavonne Mueller. Reprinted by permission of the author. Contact: Lavonne Mueller, 744 Kimberly Drive, DeKalb, IL 60115-1418

Daddy And The Tunnel Rat Copyright © 1997 by Mark Blickley. Reprinted by permission of the author. Contact: Mark Blickley, 425 Garden Street, Hoboken, NJ 07030, (201) 656-3146

Easter Copyright © 1997 by William Scheffer. Reprinted by permission of Berman, Boals & Flynn on behalf of author. CAUTION: Professionals and amateurs are hereby warned that performance of *Easter* by William Scheffer is subject to royalty. It is fully protected under the copyright laws of the United States of America, and of all countries covered by the International Copyright Union (including the Dominion of Canada and the rest of the British Commonwealth), and of all countries covered by the Pan-American

Copyright Convention and the Universal Copyright Convention, the Berne Convention and of all countries with which the United States has reciprocal copyright relations. All rights, including professional, amateur/motion picture stage rights, recitation, lecturing, public reading, radio broadcasting, television, video or sound recording, all other forms of mechanical or electronic reproduction, such as CD-ROM, CD-1, information storage and retrieval systems and photocopying, and the rights of translation into foreign languages, are strictly reserved. Particular emphasis is laid upon the matter of readings, permission for which must be obtained from the author's agent in writing. Contact: Berman, Boals & Flynn, 208 West 30th Street, #401, New York, NY 10001, Attn: Judy Boals, Author's Agent

Epic Poetry Copyright © 1997 by James Bosley. Reprinted by permission of Rosenstone/ Wender. Contact: Rosenstone/Wender, 3 East 48th Street, New York, NY 10017, (212) 832-8330, Attn: Ronald Gwiazda, Author's Agent

Feathers In The Dust Copyright © 1997 by Richard Lay. Reprinted by Permission of the author. Contact: Richard Lay, 205 West 15th Street, 2M, New York, NY 10011, (212) 929-3423

The Golem Copyright © 1997 by Andrew C. Ordover. Reprinted by permission of the author. Contact: Andrew C. Ordover, 381 1st Street, Brooklyn, NY 11215-1905, (718) 369-1766

Good Guys Wear Yellow Copyright © 1992 by Daphne R. Hull. Reprinted by permission of the author. Contact: Daphne R. Hull 841 Park Avenue, Baltimore, MD 21201 (410) 783-5729 e-mail: ink@ix.netcom.com

The Government Inspector by Nikolai Gogol, new adaptation copyright © 1997 by Philip Goulding. Reprinted by permission of the author. Contact: Eric Glass, Ltd., 28 Berkeley Square, London W1X 6HD, UK

Hazing The Monkey Copyright © 1996 by Marcus A. Hennessy. Reprinted by Permission of the author. Contact: Marcus A. Hennessy, 827 9th Street, #6, Santa Monica, CA 90403

Icarus Copyright © 1997 by Edward Sanchez. Reprinted by permission of the author. CAUTION: Professionals and amateurs are hereby warned that performance of *Icarus* is subject to royalty. It is fully protected under the copyright laws of the United States of America, and of all countries covered by the International Copyright Union (including the Dominion of Canada and the rest of the British Commonwealth), and of all countries covered by the Pan American Copyright Convention and the Universal Copyright Convention, the Berne Convention and of all countries with which the United States has reciprocal copyright relations. All rights, including professional, amateur/motion picture stage rights, recitation, lecturing, public reading, radio broadcasting, television, video or sound recording, all other forms of mechanical or electronic reproduction, such as CD-ROM, CD-1, information storage and retrieval systems and photocopying, and the rights of translation into foreign languages, are strictly reserved. Particular emphasis is laid upon the matter of readings, permission for which must be obtained from the author's agent in writing. Contact: The Joyce Ketay Agency, 1501 Broadway, Suite 1908, New York, NY 10036, Attn: Carl Mulert, Author's Agent

In Search Of The Red River Dog Copyright © 1997 by Sandra Perlman, all rights reserved. Reprinted by permission of the author. Contact: Sandra Perlman, 429 Carthage Avenue, Kent, OH 44240

145